The
PUBLIC SCHOOL
and the
PRIVATE VISION

*A Search for America
in Education and Literature*

MAXINE GREENE

THE NEW PRESS

NEW YORK
LONDON

Requests for permission to reproduce selections from this book should be mailed to:
Permissions Department, The New Press, 38 Greene Street, New York, NY 10013.

Originally published by Random House, Inc, New York, 1965
This edition published in the United States by The New Press, New York, 2007
Distributed by W. W. Norton & Company, Inc., New York

ISBN 978-1-59558-153-2 (pbk)
ISBN 978-1-59558-182-2 (hc)
CIP data available

The New Press was established in 1990 as a not-for-profit alternative to the large,
commercial publishing houses currently dominating the book publishing industry.
The New Press operates in the public interest rather than for private gain, and is
committed to publishing, in innovative ways, works of educational, cultural, and
community value that are often deemed insufficiently profitable.

www.thenewpress.com

Composition by NK Graphics/A Black Dot Group Company
This book was set in New Caledonia

Printed in Canada

2   4   6   8   10   9   7   5   3   1

FOR
Linda and Tim

Contents

The

PUBLIC SCHOOL

and the

PRIVATE VISION

SERIES FOREWORD
Classics in
Progressive Education

My first classroom was empty. Not a book, piece of paper, pencil, or stick of chalk was in sight. The principal welcomed me to the school and informed me he had high expectations for each and every student. Crazy. I figured I had to dig into my meager savings and buy pencils, some remaindered typing paper, and discount crayons. Books were out of the question.

It was rough going for my first week of teaching, but during my second, two older female teachers showed up in my classroom after school. It turns out they were watching me and decided I might be a lifer—a life-long progressive education teacher. They brought me boxes of books, material about the United Federation of Teachers, and most of all, some classics of progressive education. Over coffee after school one day, they informed me that both of them would retire in a year but wanted to keep the tradition of democratic, student-centered education alive. These teachers hoped to keep arts in the schools and they hoped that young teachers like me (I was 23 at the time) would keep the tradition going. But, they emphasized, in order to keep a tradition alive, you had to know its history and read its literature. That's why, in addition to all the specific educational material these teachers brought me, they insisted I read Dewey, Froebel, Freinet, Homer Lane, Makarenko, and many other democratic educators whose work has had major influences on educators throughout the world. Their teaching was concrete and their vision for education was large.

I didn't have a chance to thank these two teachers because they retired in the middle of my first year of teaching without leaving their names or addresses. But I have honored their commitment to children and to progressive education. This series is meant to show them my appreciation for their unsolicited gifts to me.

This series will reissue important but often hard-to-find works of progressive education which are still very useful to people teaching today. It is essential to connect to tradition, to know that you are not alone trying to fight against authoritarian or corporate education. The goal is to energize teachers through a connection to educators who have struggled for democratic and creative education against the demands of governments, the rigidity of some churches, and the complex lives many students are forced to bear. The books reprinted are for teachers of hope who understand the complexities of struggling for their students and who might need a dose of history, a bit of humor, and lots of new ideas.

—Herbert Kohl
February 2007

Foreword

Maxine Greene, one of the leading educational philosophers of the past fifty years, remains "an idol to thousands of educators," according to the *New York Times*. In *The Public School and the Private Vision*, initially published in 1965 and with a new preface by the author especially for this edition, Maxine traces the complex interplay of literature and public education from the 1830s to the 1960s. With rare eloquence she affirms the values that lie at the root of public education—perhaps the most emblematic symbol of an egalitarian American society—and makes a call for decency in difficult times.

At a time when we are once again asking ourselves questions such as "Education for whom?" and "Education for what?" Maxine's book reminds us that these questions have never had easy answers. The answers provided by the visionaries who dreamed up the free public education experiment in the early nineteenth century, as well as by reformers over the intervening two hundred years, were products of their times, and their visions for schools were informed by the social contexts in which they worked.

For this reason, Maxine has found it instructive to compare the values and goals of school reformers—from Thomas Jefferson and Horace Mann to McGuffey and John Dewey—with the ideals and critiques set forth in more nuanced ways by literary writers of the same eras. It is often via works of fiction and creative writing that a society can test and explore its most cherished beliefs—a luxury not afforded many educators, reformers, and practitioners on the ground.

The Public School and the Private Vision takes the novel approach of using classics of literary writing to shed light on the changing shapes of American culture and the evolution of American ideals since the founding of the common schools in 1837. The common schools were the first free public schools in the United States. They introduced the at-that-time radical idea that all children are entitled to a free education. Unfortunately, at the same time African Americans were excluded in many states since they were enslaved, and education for slaves' children was considered a danger to the whole system of slavery.

An educated people were, and still are, considered a danger, not to democracy, but to the wealthy who profit from other people's labor. In Maxine's book the rhetoric and convictions of the school reformers over the years are presented in counterpoint to the perspectives of writers at approximately the same places at the same time, from Nathaniel Hawthorne and Thoreau, through Melville, Mark Twain, F. Scott Fitzgerald, and Ralph Ellison. The point is not that literary men and women commented directly on the schools, although they may have done so indirectly on the processes of education. It is, rather, that writers were likely to bring to the surface values, ambiguities, and unanswered questions relevant to schools but either ignored or unspoken by reformers preoccupied with literacy and social change.

The counterpoint between the writers' critique and the utopian work of educators are at the heart of this book. What makes it important for us now is that the same dissonance exists. Societies require visionaries with lofty ideals, including universal education. They also require self-critique. The struggle to reconcile these competing visions—the tension between "reformers" and "writers" (understanding that in real life these terms are seldom mutually exclusive)—can once again prove instructive in guiding us through today's turbulent school-reform waters.

In a recent conversation with Maxine Green she referred to her life as an uncompleted project. We had been talking about Jean-Paul Sartre, who is one of my heroes and someone whose work she has studied with a passion. Passion and Maxine go together. There is no one else I know whose life and work so embodies intellectual passion and the practice of love.

The practice of love requires an understanding of uncompleted projects. Incompleteness is as important and positive an idea as its opposite, completeness, though it is hardly ever considered that way. The idea of completion is a positive value in school and society. You're supposed to finish what you begin, carry through something to its end, do an exhibition of what you learned that summarizes and completes your learning. If you start something you're supposed to stick to it to the end. If you don't complete a book you start or finish a project or get all your credits in schools or turn in all of your assignments, there's something wrong with you. You are irresponsible, lazy, and unreliable.

I have learned how to complete things but must admit that the most interesting things I've ever tried to do have never been finished. Some have been put on hold; others have been abandoned. And a few are still in my mind, floating about, still interesting in some ways and yet not compelling enough or clear enough to be brought to the surface and completed.

The limitations of system-building is part of what Maxine describes in this book: a dialogue between the writer and the teacher, an uneasy one, but a very productive one for those of us who choose to work with young people.

Maxine understands that metaphor and writing are tools for the social imagination. One of the centers of Maxine's life and work (and they are not distinguishable) whether it is in kindergarten or graduate school, is the development of a sensitive and compassionate social imagination. This is another way of saying that Maxine is a practical dreamer, a radical utopian, a person who, while fully understanding current social, economic, and political realities, has a vision of a more decent way of organizing human life and society.

This vision, being both artistic and utopian, is not limited by arguments that cite "the way the world is" or "human nature."

For Maxine human nature is made, not fixed, and the literary vision of a decent world, or the sensibility that criticizes it, serve to extend people's notion of the possible.

Some people shy away from incompleteness and make their dreams and projects small. Others gamble on winning and walking away from things. But Maxine, true existential dreamer, embraces the uncompleted project that is her life. She dreams big and the dream stays alive.

—Herbert Kohl
February 2007

Preface

Written in the 1960s and reexamined in a different intellectual climate, this book takes a look from several points of view at the changing shape of American culture since the founding of the common schools in 1837. The rhetoric and convictions of the school reformers over the years are presented in counterpoint to the perspectives of imaginative writers finding expression in approximately the same places at the same time. The point is not that literary men and women commented directly on the schools, although they may have done so (indirectly) on the processes of education. It is, rather, that imaginative writers were likely to bring to the surface values, ambiguities, and unanswered questions relevant to schools but either ignored or unspoken by so-called reformers preoccupied with elementary literacy, social control, and "voluntary compliance" with moral laws.

Bringing forward such figures as Bartleby who "preferred not to" comply with what was taken for granted as appropriate behavior; Huck Finn who felt "all cramped up" in a slave society whose mores he was unable to question and which compelled him to "pray a lie" for what modern readers know is the good; and Hester Prynne who looked at the order of things "as if through the eyes of a wild Indian," I found it important to call attention to human particularity and vibrancy. Because I was writing in the Sixties, I found such attitudes not only reflective of a moment in educational and social history, but in some manner prophetic. I had in mind an emancipatory moment on the horizon actually prepared for and justified by what the characters in a few artists' invented worlds were making articulate.

Writing in the new century, I would have considered what has been made clear in the debates about history and the history of ideas—whether or not there is a direction to history, whether trends and predictions and personal insights infuse meaning into the course of events. I would have dealt in more detail with the relations between fictions and "reality." And, surely, I would have taken into account the growing influence of the measurable in educational thought and practice, the persistence of learning curves, the influence of eugenics, the dependence on testing, the reliance on extrinsic standards, and the blight of "savage inequalities."

There may be hope to be found in the challenges now being raised to the congealing of evangelism and radical right-wing thinking as they have affected the schools. There may be hope to be found in the appearance of small schools, the interest in teaching as a fostering of dialogue and a search for meaning responsive to diversity and difference. There may be hope in the naming of social justice as a fundamental concern of the public school, and in the opening of schools as a public space where individuals may come together in their pursuit of freedom and connectedness.

The opening of untapped possibilities through the exercise of imagination still seems important to me, even as I realize how necessary it is today to disclose the terrors so often suppressed in human consciousness. I would affirm my confidence as never before in the new beginnings implicit in the educational undertaking. So long as we remember that education has to do with the young in their unpredictable becoming, so long as we can free ourselves from today's "iron cage" of technicist manipulation and control, we may be able to illuminate the public school with a vision arising from the "community in the making" John Dewey called "democracy."

—Maxine Greene
January 2007

1

THE SEARCH BEGINS
Education, Literature,
and the Dream

When, in the early nineteenth century, campaigns for public education began in America, the men who argued the cause of common schools linked them to the ancestral Promise and to the images of the American Dream. Not only would the schools, they said, provide a common experience and a common heritage for the diverse children of the nation, they would also equip the young for the responsibilities of freedom, insure universal equality, and guarantee prosperity through the years to come. In sum, the reformers were telling the world, free schools would provide the bricks and mortar for the Heavenly City on earth.

It is difficult today to feel the ardor and the urgency of that rhetoric, since now the public schools are thought of as part of the nature of things. They conduct a complicated, unheroic business; and, although men battle recurrently over what is called their inadequacy, they seem to have been always with us, "too much with us, late and soon." We forget how problematic they were a century ago. We forget that the controversies they aroused were controversies not about schools alone, but about the validity of the claim that a community of common men could be created in an open world—and that it could survive.

The schools' beginnings coincided with the beginnings of an authentic American imaginative literature, with the earliest efforts to give American experience significant form in art. Although the "renaissance" was greeted as a bright awakening by Ralph Waldo Emerson, the writers who began telling American tales were, almost without exception, men with "dark" perceptions of life. At the very moment the school reformers were speaking their rhetoric of assurance and hope, the artists were writing of ambiguities, of human impotence and fallibility, of wildernesses, wastes, dualities. Yet they lived in the same world and breathed the same free air.

The "meaning" of that world—of any world—depends on the way it is seen, conceptualized, formed. Schoolmen and artists both must organize their experience and make sense of it for themselves. The principle or the mode of organization will vary with temperament, capacity, style of life, and end in view. Some will seek out man's condition under the sky; others will visualize men in relationship, making their laws, achieving their practical goals. Some will see darkness overtaking the light; others will find it sensible only to work in the day. Some will deal in presentations, in efforts to make people feel and form; others will work with fact and truth, informing, making people know. And, at any given moment of history, the "reality" which is defined is in some sense equivalent to the multiple ways in which experience has been formed.

So it is with social reality as it plays upon the schools. The schools, particularly in America, have been inseparable from the matrix of cultural life since the earliest days of settlement. Initially, this was because of the differences among the colonies and the widespread defensiveness with respect to group identity. The Moravians therefore affirmed their very substance when they sent their children to their own parochial schools; the Puritans of the Massachusetts Bay Colony did the same when they enacted the "Olde Deluder Satan" Act, requiring every child to learn the catechism, the capital laws, and the rudiments of a trade. The Southern Anglicans, relying on tutors for the rich and charity instruction for the poor, were deliberately perpetuating the English way of life; the colonists in New Amsterdam, with their Reformed Church schools, continued in the Dutch way.

During the eighteenth century, the strands began to interweave, as the *American* with American problems appeared. But when Benjamin Franklin worked out his plan for "the Education of Youth in Pennsylvania," he gave utilitarian training far more weight than middle-class prejudices would allow, in spite of middle-class need; and European formal training overcame the Franklin design. Thomas Jefferson was in advance of public opinion when he introduced his proposal for free schools in Virginia; and, because of the nature of the cultural matrix at the moment, his ideas aroused no response.

Widespread entanglement of educational proposals with the fabric of cultural feelings and beliefs became even more apparent when Jackson was elected President, and the opinions of the common men had to be taken into account. Horace Mann's successes, like those of other educational reformers, were largely due to his awareness of what the people he addressed were thinking, what they believed the changes around them would mean, what they understood when men talked about the significance of a common school.

The effort to discover the meanings in the history of that school, however, involves more than a consideration of the rhetoric of prophetic crusaders like Mann. He liked to explain that it was "a great, immutable principle of natural law or natural ethics . . . a principle of divine origin, clearly legible in the ways of Providence as those ways are manifested in the order of nature and in the history of the race—which proves the absolute right of every human being that comes into the world to an education. . . ." The same principle, he said, "proves the correlative duty of every government to see that the means of that education are provided for all." It was self-evident that, since the American Republic was founded in accordance with natural law, the state governments would have to do their duty and establish the "means of education" for all—universal public schools.

Clearly this sort of rationale, strategically successful though it was, is unwarranted from the twentieth-century point of view. Contemporary educators cannot refer to the "ways of Providence" or to some self-existent "natural ethic" when defending the claims of tax-supported schools. Nevertheless, it is important to keep in mind that there are multiple ways of seeking justification for one's belief—and that even Mann's vision of what he called "reality," shared by many of his contemporaries though it was, did not encompass all the meanings in the culture surrounding the schools of his day. This is why the coming chapters will attempt to enable readers in search of historic meaning to see through perspectives alternative to Mann's, to consider from a variety of vantage points the story of the common schools.

Each of the vantage points to be taken will have the capacity to reveal something new. The literary view will be frequently chosen, however, as a foil for the view created by the rhetoric of the common school champions. This will be so because the literary artist is characteristically concerned with presenting his personal experience of life, his individual confrontations with tension and change. Also, he is concerned with identifying the insufficiencies he feels, the discrepancies between existence and prevalent descriptions of it, the strains of contesting values and ideals. Unlike the reformer or the orator, he is given to perceiving conflict dramatically. It is his object to integrate his materials imaginatively, to achieve aesthetic resolutions rather than social change or effective persuasion; and he attempts to do this by exploring, probing, molding the particulars he forms.

There is a sense in which the educator is doing the same, but in another discursive dimension, where general tendencies are dealt with, logical relations effected, inferences drawn, conclusions derived. It is as if the reformers have chosen to stand on high places, looking over the heads of the illiterate and disinherited through the glass of reason and warranted possibility. Standing there, they have envisaged and described an educational enterprise that is the mainstay of the Republic, the guarantee of human rights, the armature of an enlightened way of life. And, saying, they have made it—in abstracto—compelling and altogether real.

The artists—Hawthorne, Thoreau, Melville, and the others—stand below in the midst of the field. They stand with individual profiles and jutting shoulders in view; they press against the human creatures listening, feeling their pulse, their warmth, their

chill. The words *Republic*, *rights*, *enlightened*, even *liberty*, hold
different meanings for individual men, if they are meaningful at
all. And the "meaning" of the whole, in this case the "meaning"
of the history of common schools, can only be fully defined if we
account for what they also hear and see.

Our movement, in the chapters to come, will be chronological in
a broad sense, beginning with the 1830s, when the common-
school campaigns began and when an American literature was
first taking form. We will recall what the school has appeared to
be at various stages of its growth and in its shifting relationship to
other activities in the American scene. We will take note of the
record as we move along, heeding the large articulations in our
history, the main currents and some tributary streams.

And, as we move, we will consider certain works of literature
as occasions for our questioning—personal questioning in the last
analysis, but occasions which may nevertheless be highlighted
and described. It is recognized that no amount of talking about a
work of art can be equivalent to a direct encounter with what it
is and what it does. And no amount of description can exhaust
the levels of experience each work has the capacity to touch. There
will remain, when the exploration is done, the manifold life lived
by the novels, poems, and stories we confront. There will remain,
to some extent unanswered, the question of what particular works
may be refracting, of the stuff being used to create the illusioned
worlds.

We will come repeatedly upon negations and affirmations,
problematic areas and certainties, expressions of despair and
high-hearted expressions of delight. Pursuing many sorts of
meaning under an arch of fact, we will continuously seek the angles of vision that may help us see the school somewhat more
clearly and understand a little more about its role in American
life. What we find will not always be demonstrable; we will seldom be conclusive about what we discover as we move. We may
be like observers in the chamber of a camera obscura, watching
the lens at one end cast an image on the screen at the other. Like

such observers, we may find that, because the tent is dark, the images of the world outside—or above—are so distinct as to show forth forms and interrelationships indistinguishable in the daylight beyond the tent. This does not mean that the projected images are more "real" than what is out there in the sun. It simply means that we can see in new ways in the darkness—and that the outside world may never be quite the same again.

Looking through the lens in the darkness, looking about in the sun, we will move through a century of history, and our certainties will diminish as we move. Simplistic descriptions will recede; facts will arrange themselves in new designs. Pursuing our questions, our uncertainties, we may find a kind of freedom in our explorations of educational history in America, the freedom that accompanies fresh perceptions and the touch of possibility. We will move backward in time at first; then we will move forward in our effort to rediscover the meanings in the past and to rediscover something of ourselves . . . "boats against the current," as Scott Fitzgerald wrote, "borne back ceaselessly. . . ." Borne back, this time, to envisage that bearer of our dreams and doubts and identities—the often shiftless, the strangely quixotic American common school.

2

ENLIGHTENMENT IDEALS AND "COMMON MEN"
From Jefferson to Mann

Thomas Jefferson broke the trail for the advance of universal education in America when he introduced a bill in the Virginia legislature in 1779. The bill called for the establishment of a state-wide system of schools for the sake of a "more general diffusion of knowledge" among Virginia's citizens. Breaking as it did with the "voluntary" tradition, the proposal seemed too radical for the time, and the bill's defeat convinced Jefferson he should wait until the people were better prepared.

It was to take more than half a century before most of the states in the Union would accept the principles of tax support and equal educational opportunity. Virginia was not alone in putting off the day when the poor as well as the rich could expect to be schooled without the humiliations of charity. The federal Constitution had said nothing on the subject. Few people saw any connection between the health of the Republic and schooling for the many, schooling that was adequate and free. Now and then, voices were raised: Benjamin Rush's, for instance; Robert Coram's. Now and then, virtue was publicly linked to literacy. But the trail once broken by Jefferson remained untraveled for many years.

Then, suddenly, in 1814, Jefferson himself took up the spade again. He had been elected to the board of trustees of Albermarle Academy, soon to be transformed into the University of Virginia. Once thrust back into the educational arena, he could not restrain himself from speaking out on public schools. Making his fellow trustee Peter Carr the "depository" of his ideas, he wrote:

> It is highly interesting to our country, and it is the duty of its functionaries, to provide that every citizen in it should receive an education proportioned to the conditions and pursuits of his life. The mass of our citizens may be divided into two classes—the laboring and the learned. The laboring will need the first grade of education to qualify for their pursuits and duties; the learned will need it as a foundation for further acquirements.

With the voice and style of the eighteenth century, Jefferson was again demanding selective education and, at once, free schools for all.

His focal concern was what it had been in the days of the founding: to preserve the Republic and to defend the rights of man. As in 1779, he was preoccupied with the necessity of avoiding tyranny. He still thought that the way to do so was "to illuminate, as far as practicable, the minds of the people at large. . . ." Freedom and republican institutions, he believed, could only survive if the people chose the wisest and most excellent among them to rule. Leaders "whom nature hath endowed with genius and virtue" would only be selected, however, if the people were schooled—enlightened enough to recognize "ambition," educated enough to learn from the experience of countries which had fallen to tyranny in the past.

This meant that the ordinary individual needed but a few years of schooling, enough to equip him to do his life's work and perform the duties of citizenship. The extraordinary, gifted individual, on the other hand, was entitled to many more years of training if he were to represent the mass of people in government. He had to be "rendered by liberal education worthy to receive, and able to safeguard the sacred deposit of the rights and liberties of [his] fellow-citizens. . . ."

In the interests of freedom, then, Jefferson was proposing a dual school system, resembling the class systems abroad. The difference was that he was not thinking of selection in terms of wealth or pedigree; nor did he have in mind the "Pseudo-Aristocracy" of the rich and well-born. Those chosen for advanced education were to be chosen on the basis of endowment and merit alone. They were to compose a "natural aristocracy" of talent, the fruits of which were to benefit the whole.

The Enlightenment concept of republicanism justified this proposal for a common *and* an un-common school. The ideal of a Republic governed it, a Republic ruled by free-born philosopher-kings. Jefferson had the arrangements of the previous century in mind, those that depended on a gentlemanly balance of political forces, not parties contesting for power. He had in mind the rational consensus which had seemed to underlay the contests of his day, the agreements on core values which had counteracted "special interest" and overcome "factionalism" with good sense.

Within a few years after Jefferson's letter to Carr, however, the traditional arrangements were being completely overturned. The population was increasing. New states had joined the Union. Suddenly there were mass political coalitions, politicians instead of statesmen, "democratic" techniques of caucus, patronage, direct election. The Western states had embodied provisions for universal white manhood suffrage in their constitutions; the original states were removing property requirements from their franchise laws. This meant that the masses—"King Numbers"—were voting for the first time and, often, for candidates of their own. It meant that men with but a rudimentary education, workingmen, propertyless men, held the balance of power, that criteria of selection had to be adapted so that the plain, the "common" man would have a chance to rule.

Jefferson died in 1826, just before the "age of the common man" was officially ushered in. He died in the year of the Jubilee, fifty years after Independence; and it is part of the American legend that his old adversary John Adams died on the same day, July 4, 1826. They had become friends in their old age; together they personified not merely the antagonisms of the eighteenth century, but also the "balance" of the post-Revolutionary days.

They were "democrat" and "aristocrat" in the sense of the past, and it was a breaking point for their countrymen when they died. The forms of the Enlightenment seemed finally shattered. The way was open for something rough, "romantic," new.

In 1828, the newly constituted Democratic Party swept Andrew Jackson into office on a platform reminiscent of Jefferson's in time past. These Democrats, too, were opposed to centralized power, to the business interests, "Federalism," and the Bank. Their coalition of mechanics, farmers, and shopkeepers was committed to defend popular rights and liberties against the heirs of the Adamses—the Whigs. When the crowds swarmed into Washington for Jackson's inauguration, Jefferson's ideas were already in the process of being remade and claimed as the plain people's own. The Man of Reason, the classicist, the gentleman farmer gave way to the champion of freeholders, the fighter for "publick happiness" and the rights of man. "All eyes are opened, or opening, to the rights of man," he had written ten days before his death. And his testament went on to say what every yearning common man wanted to believe:

The general spread of the light of science has already laid open to every view the palpable truth that the mass of mankind has not been born with saddles on their backs, nor a favored few booted and spurred, ready to ride them legitimately, by the grace of God. There are grounds of hope for others.

Just as the mechanics and farmers found it possible to project their own Jefferson, so did many of those concerned about education. Educational themes were woven throughout Jefferson's body of work; images of light recurred in many contexts; images of the "mass" and the "grounds of hope." There were some who saw intimations of common schools, not public schools alone. What would come closer to the Jeffersonian dream in an age of common men? What surer way was there of keeping such men unsaddled—and at once enlightened and controlled?

It was in Massachusetts that the ground was best prepared for such ideas. The Puritan town school tradition and an old commitment to "humanism" and catechisms had moved the lawmakers there to take action early. In 1789 a law had been passed giving districts the right to levy taxes in support of local schools. In 1826 each of those districts had been required to appoint a school committee to take responsibility for schools.

There were district schools by then in New York and other places, but no state had advanced so far as Massachusetts where the "general diffusion of knowledge" was concerned. Morally inspired though many of them were, no educational leaders were so well equipped to provide examples for the rest of the country. None were in a better position to integrate the Jeffersonian principles into a framework of ideas on the "common," the practical, the good.

But this did not mean that in 1828 the Massachusetts district schools were functioning effectively, or that equality of educational opportunity had finally been achieved. The districts had been given the right to make all decisions regarding school taxation, and many were too poor to support any schools at all. Others were simply not interested, especially when their largest taxpayers—and often their selectmen—customarily sent their children to private schools.

The typical district school, therefore, was no better than a charity school. Dilapidated in appearance, inept and shiftless in the service it rendered, it remained open for about two months each year. To pay for fuel and minimal repairs, fees or rate bills were commonly charged, and these excluded the children of the very poor. The school committee visited infrequently; the teacher was likely to be the neighborhood incompetent, totally unskilled. And, most often, nothing could be done, since the state had no powers of supervision or control and since, in any case, the state government offices were generally hundreds of miles away. The locality, left to its own devices, lived up to the letter of the law, and that was all. It was unusual if the parents of those who needed schooling most bothered to complain.

The schoolroom, especially in rural areas, was barren of books and equipment, with "the warping floor, the battered seats" of the schoolhouse John Greenleaf Whittier was to describe. Or, like the one in Washington Irving's Sleepy Hollow, it was "rudely constructed of logs; the windows partly glazed, and partly patched with leaves of old copy-books." The schoolmaster might be an itinerant "gentleman-like personage" like Ichabod Crane— "an odd mixture of small shrewdness and simple credulity." He might be the local sexton or bellringer, or the wastrel son of some local family. Or there might be a schoolmistress selected from among the spinsters in a town or from the young girls with poor prospects of marriage, in need of nothing more than pittances to keep themselves respectable and alive.

Conditions were scarcely better in the larger towns and the cities. Private schools and academies of all sorts were growing with the middle-class population; the town schools catered largely to the poor. The atmosphere prevailing in them was institutional and bleak. The teachers were university graduates, very often filling in the days until they found the openings they sought; or they were young theologians awaiting ordination, no more concerned than the would-be businessmen about the children they taught. Teaching was not a respectable occupation for adult men: and in any case it seemed to demand only disciplinary skills. Teachers sat on raised platforms and heard the recitations of a hundred children or more in a week. They conducted drills, saw that lessons were being memorized, kept order with hickory sticks or ferrules.

More children were being taught the skills of literacy in Massachusetts than in any other state; but there was little to be proud of, as men like James G. Carter had been saying since 1821. A Harvard graduate and teacher, Carter began by writing letters on the free schools for the Boston press. Later he published *Essays on Public Education* to sum up his account of the Massachusetts educational tradition and the sad estate of the existing schools. It was due mainly to Carter's pressure that the school committees were required by law; and it was because of his efforts that the legislature, in 1827, made taxation for the district schools compulsory.

Equally important to Carter, however, were the quality of teaching in the public schools, the books and materials made available, and what he called the "science" of education. "Instructors and pupils," he wrote, "do not understand each other. They do not speak the same language. They may use the same words; but this can hardly be called the same language, while they attach to them such very different meanings."

He therefore launched a campaign for the establishment of a teacher-training seminary, which was to be both "literary and scientific" and was to create its own literature for use in the schools, its own science of pedagogy. Although Carter hoped to see all the schools brought under state control, he thought it most important for teacher training to be state-supported and state-controlled. This was because of the "influence on society" it would exert, an influence which had to be susceptible to public opinion. Public opinion, in fact, ought to control any "engine" potent enough to "sway the public sentiment, the public morals, and the public religion. . . ."

Although Carter used Jeffersonian language like "diffusion of knowledge," he departed from Jefferson's thinking with respect to which educational institutions most deserved "the public bounty." Not those concerned with placing a few scholars "upon a level with the Germans in a knowledge of Greek accents," wrote Carter mockingly, but "those which will put our whole people upon the level of enlightened men in their practical knowledge of common things. . . ." And, for him, such knowledge ranked as high as the "liberal education" Jefferson had reserved for the "natural aristocracy," the few.

Carter's campaign for public high schools was carried on in a similar vein. He challenged the surviving Grammar Schools and Classical Schools and, at once, the proliferating Academies. Catering to the few and generally to the wealthy, they seemed to him to constitute the beginnings of a "class" or dual system; and

Carter, along with other "friends of education," wanted to see a wholly common school system extending from the primary grades to the colleges, attended by all classes, providing technical, scientific, and practical skills.

This challenge to the classical tendency was more successful than the appeal for a teacher-training seminary. The state passed a law in 1827 requiring all towns of over five hundred inhabitants to establish public high schools; but Carter's petition for normal-school legislation was denied. Not until 1839 was the first normal school established in Concord; by then Carter no longer held the center of the stage.

Nonetheless he, more than anyone else, brought the struggle for a common school into the mainstream of the Jacksonian age. He laid the groundwork for the linking of public education to the rise of industry, and for the use of education as a checkrein on both "German" intellectuals and common people organized as "mobs." The campaigns he had done so much to launch widened and deepened as the 1830s began. They became a movement for enlightenment, a movement devoted to educating the people on the meaning of common schools. And it was this that made Massachusetts, like Pericles' Athens, the "school" of the larger community. Inspiring lessons on public education would be illustrated and taught; Jefferson's themes would be elaborated; and, before long, the nation would heed.

The next step forward in Massachusetts was taken in 1837. It was the year Jackson left the Presidency, the year a great economic depression began—and the year Ralph Waldo Emerson delivered the Phi Beta Kappa address at Harvard. The address was called "The American Scholar," and Oliver Wendell Holmes was to speak of it as "our intellectual Declaration of Independence." Emerson's concerns were American literature and American thought; but what he said held implications for education as well—particularly the indigenous form of education called the common school. "Our day of dependence," he told his audience, "our long apprenticeship to the learning of other lands, draws to a close. The millions, that around us are rushing into life, cannot always be fed on the sere remains of foreign harvests."

The end of "apprenticeship" was marked in the legislature by the passage of a bill creating a State Board of Education. The bill had been drafted by Carter, elected to the house two years before and soon made chairman of the Committee on Education; but the man asked to become Secretary of the Board was a Boston lawyer and legislator named Horace Mann. A descendant of Puritans, he had been converted to a belief in human improvement when he was young. On graduating from Brown University in 1819, he had delivered an oration entitled "The Gradual Advancement of the Human Species in Dignity and Happiness." Later, when he was elected to the Massachusetts legislature, he became a kind of prophet of "advancement," which he read most often as public righteousness. He espoused one campaign after another: for temperance, for railroad building, for hospitals for the insane, and, as state senator and senate president, for tax-supported schools.

When he was asked to take the post as Secretary, he responded with Old Testament fervor. "The bar is no longer my forum," he wrote to a friend. "My jurisdiction is changed. I have abandoned jurisprudence and betaken myself to the larger sphere of mind and morals." To abandon law meant giving up a profitable practice with considerable standing and security in exchange for a position with minimal power attached to it and little financial reward. The mission of the new Board was simply to inform the people of Massachusetts about the condition of their schools, not to do anything about them. Mann could look forward only to writing, speaking, and traveling around the state in the interests of the schools.

Nevertheless he greeted the appointment as an opportunity to commence a moral crusade. ("I have faith in the improvability of the race," he wrote in his diary "—in their accelerating improvability.") He could visualize himself as the champion of improvability; and the prospect was in accord with his idealism, his seriousness, and with a Calvinist conscience which conversion to Unitarianism had never undermined.

He plunged into his work as Secretary with the conviction that education was the first of all causes. No other institution seemed to offer such promise of improving and redeeming human beings. No other institution could do so much to train the young in "rational obedience," in "voluntary compliance" with what was lawful and right. "Without undervaluing any other human agency," he wrote after almost a decade as Secretary, "it may be safely affirmed that the common school, improved and energized as it can easily be, may become the most effective and benignant of all the forces of civilization."

By 1837 Massachusetts was no longer alone in the attempt to make local schools a matter of state concern. After angry campaigns against it by parochial groups, a Free School Act had finally been passed in Pennsylvania. Pauper schools were being repudiated in New Jersey. New York, which had created the first school superintendency, had abolished the office because of general indifference; but Michigan was about to install a chief state officer with powers of certification and control. Even in Tennessee, the General Assembly had passed a law calling for an *ex officio* board of education and a superintendent of public instruction.

Mann's feeling of urgency was therefore intensified by the sense that Massachusetts, for all its high literacy rate and proud tradition, was in danger of falling behind. Understandably, his first Annual Report showed signs of bitterness. He had traveled miles across the state, inspected numerous ill-kept schoolhouses in remote villages, appealed to countless grudging school committees and uninterested parents—and his reaction was outrage at the "apathy of the people themselves." His most acid comments were reserved for the well-to-do who sent their children to private schools, thus depriving their districts of desperately needed funds and the "lower classes" of all "abstract standard of excellence" without which they could not rise.

Mann directed his appeal at the conscience of those he held responsible: the respectable, middle-class parents who had long known it was their duty to take care of the poor. "Without some favoring influence to woo out and cheer their faculties," he told them, the children of those poor would remain "mere inanimate forms. . . ." He asked first for moral commitment to some "social principle"; then, as his decade in office wore on, he began appealing to his audiences in terms of expediency or special interest. He told businessmen that public schools would insure the maintenance of public order and the protection of their property. He spoke to moralists and humanitarians of the virtues of mass enlightenment, of the necessity for equality. He offered workingmen and mechanics bright visions of prosperity and status for their children in the days to come.

The "lower classes," it transpired, were the hardest of all to convince. They had believed in the visions Mann now was presenting, but they had lost the hopes that had buoyed them up during Jackson's Presidency. Then, in the early 1830s, they had banded together to speed the coming of successes presumably guaranteed by the power of their votes. They had organized craft unions or joined Workingmen's Associations in the conviction that cooperative action would protect individual autonomy. Envisaging themselves as tradesmen, entrepreneurs, they had challenged the Bank along with the farmers, defied the large trading interests, fought the competition of prison labor and slaves. They had demanded easy credit, anti-monopoly laws, and, along with these, decent public schools.

Oriented to laissez faire and to free enterprise, they had called for educational equality as a means of attaining equality with mill-owners, railroad builders, hard-money men—with all who had tried to keep "saddles on their backs." Equal educational opportunity had seemed to them a protection against class inequity; also, it had seemed to promise that their children, too, would be taught the disciplines of self-reliance and "a just disposition," as their resolutions said, "virtuous habits, . . . a rational, self-governing character. . . ."

But the depression of 1837 intervened; and, by the time Horace Mann began addressing them, their confidence was eroded. The Workingmen's Associations had already disintegrated; there seemed no point to them, once their members confronted the fact that they were fated to be mechanics and hired men after all. Nor did there seem to be any point to demands for public education—not if the schools were to serve only as training institutions, making docile citizens and workers out of children born to be journeymen.

Mann therefore found it difficult to enlist their support and difficult to arouse them from inertia. When he spoke of industrial expansion or the promise of the factories, he met blank resistance from people who had spent their lives opposing the "workshop," the mills, the financiers. It was too soon for most of them to acknowledge that something vast and impersonal—like a landslide or a flood—was altering the face of the country they knew. They chose, in their hopelessness, to put the blame on mercantilism, on the city, on the Whigs; they could not feel the momentum of the new technology, which, for Mann, was one of the arguments for schools.

They had not yet read the meaning in Eli Whitney's invention of interchangeable parts in manufactured goods, nor in the proliferation of cotton mills throughout the North. They could see no significance in the integrated cotton-manufacturing processes the Boston Manufacturing Company had installed at Waltham, Massachusetts. Like those who had visited and marveled at the operation, the workingmen thought it just a curiosity. The workers in the "model factory" were respectable, handsome New England girls, housed and educated in the company town. Grown famous for their looks and for their habit of reciting poetry at the looms, they seemed to have no connection with adult males who also had to work. Factories still were places for women and children; it was up to a man to fend for himself—preferably with a loom of his own.

As the depression continued and became world-wide, some of

the workingmen turned toward the West. Others, little by little, became convinced that factory work was all there was; and often, when they went in search of unskilled jobs, they found themselves competing with Irishmen or Lancashiremen, immigrants whose numbers were increasing year by year. There were spurts of anger in consequence, anger expressed in the burning of a convent in 1834, in the formation of the Native American Association in 1837. The common men found it increasingly hard to place much faith in schools.

They were not, therefore, the natural allies of school reformers; and Horace Mann, who was a Whig in politics, demonstrated progressively less sympathy with their outmoded dreams. His perception of what was happening in America made him disagree with such spokesmen as the historian George Bancroft, with his affirmation of faith in the common people's disinterest and natural sagacity. For Mann, human beings had to be taught to apprehend the laws of civilized behavior. The alternative was license, not a noble savagery—disorder, threats to the *status quo*. Early in 1837 there had been riots in the North, and in New York the rioters had raided food stores under signs saying "BREAD, MEAT, RENT, AND FUEL!" They had been stopped before much damage was done, but the object lesson seemed clear.

Mann told his audiences that a common school would alleviate the "revenge and the madness" of the poor. Revenge was identified with what he called "agrarianism"; and "the wanton destruction of the property of others—the burning of hay-ricks and corn-ricks, the demolition of machinery because it supersedes hand-labor, the sprinkling of vitriol on rich dresses—is only agrarianism run mad." If the children of the poor were taught to help themselves, they would be less likely to avenge themselves on others. They would possess the skills and the feeling of independence which would enable them to "resist the selfishness of other men."

Moreover, if all children went to school together and shared experiences day after day, the gulf between the classes would be narrowed, and hostility would accordingly decrease. In adult life, then, no matter what the differences among them, they would be able to look back upon a "common" life, a "common" store of experiences; and this would overcome estrangement and the sense of coming from different worlds.

The school, therefore, would not only equalize opportunity by equipping all young people to compete, it would also serve to overcome the class distinctions so alien to America; it would become "the great equalizer of the conditions of men—the balance wheel of the social machinery." Everyone, no matter how humble, would have a chance to rise. The child of the Irish millworker would grow up beside the mill-owner's child; the offspring of the most oppressed peasant immigrants would be taught the skills and principles required—and go on to take their places in the commonalty.

But there could be no commonalty, there could be no community, if there were no compliance with the "laws of reason and duty." Mann talked of voluntary obedience and conformity, not coercion; he talked of "self-government," not controls imposed from without. The rule of Right, however, was to be "made to stand out, broad, lofty, and as conspicuous as a mountain against a clear sky." To be educated was to apprehend and to accept the absoluteness of the rule. And it was not by chance that the rule called for "good habits," which it was the school's "true business" to insure.

Mann was not inclined to say, as Jefferson had, that "the care of every man's soul belongs to himself." He was not inclined to assert, as Jefferson had, that an enlightened people could be trusted to exercise their "natural powers" and, by doing so, become dignified and worthy of regard. As Mann saw it, it was not enough to *inform* the people, to acquaint them with knowledge and facts. Controls were required if they were to be trusted with the rights of citizenship. He was a Whig, a moralist, an antagonist of laissez faire; he could not but express this in his view of the schools. Jefferson had said that the best government was the one which governed least. Mann wrote: "So tremendous . . . are the evils of anarchy and lawlessness, that a government by mere force, however arbitrary and cruel, has been held preferable to no-government."

It followed that "self-government" for him—or "self-control"—was to be learned through mastery of the preexistent laws. Like most moral precepts, these laws were largely negative. For all the eighteenth-century (and Unitarian) articulation given them by Mann, they were evocative of Puritan Massachusetts in the ancestral past—or perhaps of Mann's early life. He used terms like *Right* repeatedly, and *Reason*; but he spoke as if the threat were "sin" in the religious sense, and as if it were the school's responsibility to bar the gates against temptation and vice. He often warned of the need for action to control the flood of "immoralities and crimes" which might at any moment break "over all moral barriers, destroying the securities and sanctities of life"; and there were times when this seemed to be his chief argument for support of the common school.

Like many spokesmen for education, he was imagining a type of community as he described what should be taught. Like many of the world's communities, his would be morally exclusive; in order to be admitted, children would have to learn rituals, limitations, and rules. His contribution was to suggest that all should have a chance to learn together and that, having learned, they would be entitled to admission and a try at the advantages inside.

Like James Carter, Mann was aware that the "manufactories" were rapidly becoming the dominant factor in Massachusetts' economic life. In the early years of his Secretaryship, he had little doubt that industry would increase the spread of wealth and lead to material advantages for the mass of people, the very ones who had to be convinced of the value of schools. When he talked of "good habits," then, he was not merely conforming to what he believed was moral law. He was describing behaviors required of compliant workers in factories—offering the poor and jobless what they needed to get in, assuring the owners the literate, disciplined employees they were seeking for the new production lines.

The school's "true business," then, was identical with the "great interests of society." This justified a mode of civic education that would exclude "controverted points." Teaching, Mann said, should be based upon those questions "upon which there is no dispute." It was with this in mind that, in a multisectarian society, he called for Bible reading in nonsectarian schools. There could be no dispute, he believed, about the moral teachings in the Bible, in spite of religious differences in the nation and the state. The Bible could speak for itself as a "common" source of Christian morals, which clearly had to be communicated in schools.

He did not anticipate the attack of the Catholic Church on what churchmen considered the "Protestant" Scripture and on the idea of a nonauthoritarian approach to moral education. Nor did he anticipate the outraged attack by orthodox Protestants on the very principle of nonsectarianism. They, too, could not conceive of character-training without doctrinal teaching or indoctrination in the beliefs of specific sects.

Mann's expressed faith in the potency of secular moral teaching remained as high as his faith in the institution of the school. Every time he rode one of his circuits about the state, every time he put out an issue of the *Common School Journal*, he gave expression to the conviction that the schools would turn out great men, good men—peaceful citizens; inventors; engineers; the professionals and the statesmen needed by a nation whose progress was guaranteed.

Only education could subdue the "unrestrained passions" of men; only education could create a conscience for the community. In his last Report, in 1848, he talked of "the great ocean of vice and crime," the fraud, counterfeiting, drink, arson, libel that humankind had never managed to control. And then he addressed himself "to all doubters, disbelievers, or despairers, in human progress," telling them of an experiment which still had not been properly tried:

It is an experiment which, even before its inception, offers the highest authority for its ultimate success. Its formula is intelligible to all; and it is as legible as though written in starry letters in an azure sky. It is expressed in these few and simple words:—"Train up a child in the way he should go, and when he is old, he will not depart from it."

The tone was one of overweening confidence in the Promise: the declaration was "positive," he said. "If the conditions are complied with, it makes no provision for a failure." This was how he had addressed the people of his state over the exhausting years. The almost religious power of his commitment seemed at last to have overcome taxpayer opposition, sectarianism, and even some of the numb disinterest of the propertyless and the poor.

He was aware of increasing complexities, however, when he left to take John Quincy Adams' seat in Congress. He could see the growth of investment leading to new sorts of inequality. With its population multiplying, Massachusetts seemed to him exposed to "the fatal extremes of overgrown wealth and overgrown poverty." But, he insisted, Universal Education might counteract these too in time, for it could never happen that "an intelligent and practical body of men should be permanently poor."

The voters, in any case, had become enlightened enough to provide for state supervision of the schools, state certification of teachers, and the establishment of teacher-training schools. The pitiable salaries were being raised; school terms were being lengthened; archaic district systems were being overhauled. Here and there, curricula were being expanded to include history and geography, as well as a number of practical subjects; and the number of schoolbooks was expanding as publishers began finding new markets among school committees with tax money to spend.

Mann, in all justice, could speak of "improvement," if "improvement" meant increased attendance in the schools, expanding literacy, stability. He could look into the distances and see other states beginning to move, calling on him for advice, reading his journal, his speeches, his Reports. He could step back, completing his last Report in a mood of awe:

In a social and political sense, it is a *Free* school system. It knows no distinction of rich and poor, of bond and free, or between those who, in the imperfect light of this world, are seeking, through different avenues, to reach the gate of heaven. Without money and without price, it throws open its doors, and spreads the table of its bounty, for all the children of the State. Like the sun, it shines, not only upon the good, but upon the evil, that they may become good; and, like the rain, its blessings descend, not only upon the just, but upon the unjust, that their injustice may depart from them and be known no more.

3

TRANSCENDENTALISTS, UTOPIANS, AND REFORMERS
The Challenge to "Establishment" and School

In 1839, after hearing Horace Mann deliver one of his talks, Ralph Waldo Emerson wrote in his *Journal*: "We are shut in schools . . . for ten or fifteen years, and come out at last with a bellyful of words and do not know a thing." To know, for Emerson, meant to feel his poetic imagination soar. It meant to open his soul to the "Oversoul," to see by the "Divine light of reason" with which every human being was endowed. The common school, teaching conventional or "common" habits of thought and perception, seemed to him a barrier against authenticity. The school reformers, he believed, would make impossible the "self-reliance" which alone permitted God to enter through the "private door."

If, as was likely, the school inculcated vulgar and self-serving habits, or the values associated with Trade, it would merely serve to perpetuate an inadequate society, an Establishment that was basically inhumane. The American, in consequence, would be taught to be a "dwarf." Surely, it was preferable to permit the child to use his intuition, to seek out God in Nature and so release the true Man in himself. He would learn more from the grass and weeds and trees than from the secondhand knowledge stored in books. He would become virtuous by trusting himself, by looking through his own eyes, contemplating beautiful forms and ideal models—hitching his "wagon to a star."

Emerson was saying this, writing it, publishing it in poetry and prose while Horace Mann was arguing the educational cause throughout the state. They inhabited the same world. They spoke, often, to the same people. And, for all the differences between them, they drew their nourishment from a common source.

The eighteenth-century tradition had been the seedbed for ideas that grew like fruit in many shapes and hues. Jonathan Edwards, early in the century, cultivated some of them, creating the hybrids of the Great Awakening: Calvinism and a "religion of the heart." Benjamin Franklin nurtured others; John Adams, Thomas Jefferson, Tom Paine, a hundred others. Then, in the Jacksonian period, there was a time of fertilizing and transplantation; but the roots remained, as did the soil.

There were the ideas of "utility" and "self-realization," intertwined with a belief in progress and in arrival at a goal. There were the variant notions about the "moral nature" of man, about his potency and freedom and his protean inner world. And there was the idea of human dignity, of the "worth" of individuality. For some, human worth was a "given," a gift from God, to be found wherever there was human liberty.

Jefferson himself had grounded his faith in people in a belief in innate "moral sense." He did not believe the peasant was wiser than the philosopher, but he did accept the idea that the plain man (untrammeled by "artificial rules") could be depended on to "know" what was right. It was because that man might become corrupted if he lost his freedom, lived in crowded cities, or was not permitted to speak as he chose that he required representation by the liberally educated "natural aristocracy." Without such an aristocracy of statesmen to guard them, the rights of men could never be secured. Deprived of those rights, as men had so often been deprived through history, Americans might become automatons or "subjects"; they might begin to resemble the masses Jefferson had seen abroad, the dehumanized *canaille*.

Both Mann and Emerson, therefore, were working in the matrix of tradition when they placed their stress on moral or spiritual development rather than on intellectual excellence. But while Mann moved *behind* Jefferson, as it were, to the heritage of Edwards and the Puritans, Emerson moved ahead to the Romantics and into a mystique of the "common man." Samuel Taylor Coleridge's doctrine of the shaping imagination appealed to him; so did the Idealists with their immanent Divine, their communion of souls, their sense that the spirit of man and the World Spirit were one. The Romantic worship of Nature, of children and men of the fields, seemed to accord with what was stirring in America, with the people "rushing into life."

Emerson spoke of the "near, the low, the common," waiting to be explored, and he suffused his conception of democratic realizations with a kind of primitivism. This brought him close to the position of George Bancroft, the historian who had campaigned for Andrew Jackson as the "unlettered man of the West," the farmer "unversed in books," bearing wisdom from the forest to the Presidency. Like James Fenimore Cooper's Natty Bumppo, the exemplary American hero was becoming one rich in "natural wisdom" undefiled by bookish knowledge; and it began to appear to the artists, at least, that formal schooling could only shackle such a man.

The men who clustered around Emerson were New England's intellectuals, but they were united in their indifference to the campaigns for common schools. Nevertheless, they saw themselves as educators, bringers of the Word or of the Light. Some had come out of traditional Calvinism, as had Horace Mann; like him, they had followed William Ellery Channing into Unitarianism. They found an equable creed when they did so, a civilized religion based on "the adoration of goodness" and appealing to the mind rather than to "enthusiasm" or faith. Stress was laid on the ethical core of traditional religious doctrines. A benevolent, rational God was assumed, an eighteenth-century deity appropriate for rational men.

Before long, however, many began finding the new religion too cool in temper. The more emotional evangelical faiths drew a few away. Emerson and fellow members of the Transcendental Club began developing a new philosophy called Transcendentalism, which soon supplanted Unitarianism as their doctrine and their faith. A blend of European idealisms and Eastern mysticisms, the philosophy was defined in the course of what were called "Conversations" which involved people like Bronson Alcott, Margaret Fuller, Henry David Thoreau, Orestes Brownson, and other New England free spirits.

Emerson's was the mind that gave form to an inchoate whirl of views, and Emerson remained at its center while others wandered off on idiosyncratic roads. Those who moved in and out of the dialogue, the unending "Conversation," were, he said, reacting to "the new importance given to the single person" at their particular moment of history. A frequently expressed purpose for coming together was to protest the alienating effect of Trade upon the "single person." Emerson said, "Man shall treat with man as a sovereign state with a sovereign state—"; but this ought not, as he saw it, imply isolation of the individual or the growth of distrust between man and man.

Yet isolation and distrust were becoming characteristic of society, with competitiveness increasing and acquisitiveness driving people apart. Charles Dickens was soon to describe "the dull and gloomy character" of the population; others would comment on the "joyless striving" after wealth. Francis Grund would talk of the American's pursuit of business "not as a means of procuring for himself and his family the necessary comforts of life, but as the fountain of all human felicity." What de Tocqueville had called the "strange unrest of happy men" had become a ceaseless, nervous reaching out for "something better."

And already, in the 1830s, immigrants were arriving in the tens of thousands. Most were settling in the burgeoning cities— in the midst of what Grund called "really wicked extravagance." They were given shacks and tenements to live in; or they "huddled in low, damp, and filthy cellars, and . . . in attics which were but little if any better. . . ." When they (and their children) went to work in factories, they found themselves compelled to labor sixteen hours a day. Working conditions were abysmally bad; language difficulties and simple ignorance made union organization almost impossible. The native-born laborers fought off association with foreigners. Nativism flared; anti-Catholicism erupted in violence. Cases of assault and arson became common in cities continually plagued by gangs of uncared-for children, by the unemployed, the petty criminals, the sick.

The Transcendentalists thought that moral regeneration was required first of all. Measures had to be taken to combat materialism, self-interest, hypocrisy. As Henry James Senior was to say, a man's spiritual individuality, or his true and perfect Self, could only be released when his soul met in communion with other souls—the souls of the poor as well as of the rich. Education ought to signify regeneration—a shaking off of masks, a progressive identification with the Oversoul, the One. Existing society, as James saw it, was insufficient, a "civilization." "Community" could only be attained when the falseness and the artifices had been removed and men became free to be themselves at last.

To be themselves, the Transcendentalists believed, was to regain a lost innocence, or the inherent awareness of the Good with which every child was born. If the spirit were to regain that awareness, however, it needed serenity and the freedom of expression on which uniqueness depended. Individuality, therefore, required cultivation; it would wither if immersed in the "common" or the "mass." Perfection and self-realization were the fruits of spontaneous inner growth; and, since they could not be taught, "good habits" and "compliance" were irrelevant to true education. As Emerson put it, the truly educated person was the authentic one who "ventured to trust himself for a taskmaster," not the civilizing forces without.

He had spoken of "Man Thinking" in his 1837 lecture and said that the thoughtful, spiritual man would not appear among "those on whom systems of education have exhausted their culture. . . ." Imaginative, original, poetic, he would arise out of "unhandselled savage nature," relying on his own intuitions, his own ability "to build the new. . . ." In years to come, Emerson was to admit that the common school was an expression of popular democracy; but he was never deeply concerned with the "popular," for all his interest in what he called the "common" and the "low." Nor was he ever to be convinced that social institutions were superior to Nature when it came to the liberation of a self-reliant man.

Some of his friends were attracted to humanitarian activity as a means of achieving communion. They joined organizations working for prison reform, women's rights, world peace, the freeing of the slaves; but Emerson was as cool to these as he was to the idea of founding Utopias for unregenerate men. He was prone to mock all excesses of reform—"the fertility of projects for the salvation of the world." In an address in 1844, he pointed sardonically to the apostles of rural living, vegetarianism, unleavened bread, to "the adepts of hominopathy, of hydropathy, of mesmerism, of phrenology. . . ." Humanity could gain nothing "whilst a man, not himself renovated, attempts to renovate things around him. . . ." The reformer, neglectful of his own authentic soul, might become "tediously good" in a single domain and narrow or careless in others; and, as Emerson perceived the life of reform, "hypocrisy and vanity are often the disgusting result." When some of his closest companions formed the colony of Brook Farm, he was equally skeptical; his response was to remain unconnected, interested, and amused.

Many of the "tediously good" were, of course, evangelists or members of one of the proliferating sects. Beckoning toward an impending Judgment Day, they were often philanthropic in their efforts to convert; and they were frequently caught up in great crusades. Sometimes they distributed Bibles throughout the countryside; sometimes they proselytized among the Indians; occasionally they did good works among prostitutes and alcoholics, or among the city poor. With the exception of the Methodists among them, they were generally opponents of the common schools. Public education constituted a threat to faith and to parochialism; and, for the German-speaking sects, it seemed a threat to cultural identity. The familiar, unlettered preachers were preferable, the simple pastors with their scorn of "book-larnin'," the mystics unspoiled by universities.

Evangelists joined forces with Transcendentalists on questions involving inequity or inhumanity to the helpless and the young. They came together most notably when the cotton industry began booming in the North with the extension of slavery in the South. Abolitionism developed almost as soon as news arrived of the plantation system and a resurgence of Southern interest in African slaves. William Lloyd Garrison, editor of *The Liberator*, and the Reverend Elijah Lovejoy of Illinois, both evangelists, saw in slavery a primarily moral issue, to be resolved by appeals to men's consciences and hearts. "I *will* be as harsh as truth, and as uncompromising as justice," wrote Garrison as he launched what would become a long career of bitter and sometimes violent appeals. He was successful in bringing the plight of the Negroes to the attention of the North, and it was largely due to him that the New England Anti-Slavery Society was formed. It quickly attracted various Transcendentalists, who acted on their own unique commitment to the cause of human flowering and human rights. Seldom as militant as Garrison or the Midwestern Abolitionists, they engaged in a constantly expanding Conversation and involved intellectuals in the North and the East. For such people, too, slavery was a predominantly moral issue. They were seldom concerned with its economic implications, with its meaning for free labor, or with the fate of individual Negroes in times to come.

Horace Mann was among the first to demonstrate awareness of the Abolitionist movement's economic overtones. He barred antislavery as a topic of discussion in the schools because, he said, politics was to be kept out of classrooms, and Abolition was a political cause. Also, it was a cause associated with violence. (Lovejoy was murdered in Illinois the year Mann was appointed to the Board.) The main reason, however, was that Massachusetts business was thriving as a result of expanded cotton-planting. The mills were beginning to hum as never before; the banks and the shipping interests were profiting from shipments of cotton to British factory towns. The schools were dependent on businessmen's taxes. Their very growth depended on businessmen's support. Mann was not inclined to antagonize business or to alienate the legislature by associating the schools with condemnations of slavery. He discouraged normal-school students from attending Abolitionist meetings. He once penalized a normal-school principal for involving himself and encouraging students to do the same.

When Mann left the school system for Congress, however, he soon came out publicly for the antislavery cause. It then became evident that the fact of slavery had been moving him to qualify his claims for Universal Education. He confessed to doubts about the schools' capability when it came to teaching human beings to "abhor oppression of their fellow men." This brought him somewhat closer to the reformers and the dissidents; but, even when he was challenging the Fugitive Slave Bill on the floor of Congress, he was not to go the way of those who challenged fundamental premises.

He remained a schoolman, committed—along with the other school reformers—to improving the existing community. Assenting to its institutions, an educational campaigner began with arguments for equality *within* the *status quo*. He justified such arguments with talk of opportunity as well as skills and habits of efficiency; and everything he promised was contingent upon "Trade." Expansion was acclaimed, therefore; progress was called valuable, even when it affected people as blind and brutal change. Because the cities meant employment, and because employment demanded literacy, urbanization also was supported. The mood of striving after success was associated with respectability. De Tocqueville, quailing before acquisitiveness, had written of the passions of ambitious men, and of how necessary it was for them to develop "strictly regular habits and a long routine of petty uniform acts." The school reformers saw still further justification in his equating of desire, discipline, and success.

There were alternative patterns of fulfillment; but they could be acted upon, it seemed, only by those who rejected the major premises of American cultural life. Numerous rebels and dissidents wholly rejected them and did not consider doing anything to improve or remake what prevailed. Instead, they became Utopians and re-enacted the voyage of their ancestors. They were frequently men capable of compassion and outrage at the sight of suffering; but they were irreconcilables, and they went in search of Promised Lands.

Every free man, they asserted, had the right to move on. They were simply claiming their right to withdraw from existing society and build a more rational community somewhere else. Two hundred or more Utopias were founded during the nineteenth century, each significantly different from the society left behind. Most were communal, with economies based on farming and handicrafts. All were on the outskirts somewhere; on the edges of the townships or in the sparsely settled territories. Challenging industry, competitiveness, and what De Tocqueville had called "disintegrative individualism," each was governed by a social principle derived from some religious or secular faith.

Their antecedents were the Moravian and Shaker colonies of the preceding centuries. Some were evangelical, as in the old days. Others were Fourierist Phalanxes, socialist in structure, oriented toward primitive (or Christian) communism. There was Etienne Cabet's Icaria; there was the socialist experiment at Nauvoo, Illinois. There was the colony purchased from the Rappite group of utopians by Robert Owen, the humanitarian idealist from Scotland. Like Owen's settlement, New Harmony, a number were initiated by immigrants and exiles but populated by Americans—people discontented with prevailing institutions, committed to beginning again.

Like the first settlers who had come to America, they moved out to their ideal communities with confidence and high hope. They were proud, as proud as tragic heroes; and when they failed, as they always did, they had to try to recognize that human fallibility had destroyed them, just as it destroyed the legendary Greeks who had tried to be equal to the gods.

So the commonwealths rose and fell; but, in the course of each one's history, designs for living and educating were put to the test repeatedly, and some were to be significant for the time to come.

New Harmony was exemplary in this respect because Robert Owen came deliberately to try out a "New System of Society" and the educational ideas he had already applied to the teaching of the Scottish poor. He arrived in 1824 and issued invitations to all those sympathetic to the cause of "mental liberty" to come to Indiana and join New Harmony. More than nine hundred free-thinking radicals, intellectuals, and workingmen responded, with, as Owen's son was to say, "a sprinkling of unprincipled sharpers thrown in."

Joseph Neef of Philadelphia was asked to administer the colony's schools. Owen had invited him because Neef had been a student and disciple of Johann Pestalozzi, whose work had originally inspired Owen to experiment with classes for workers' children. Neef, with William Maclure, geologist and fellow-Pestalozzian, set up a New Harmony educational system with dispatch; and Neef before long published an exact account of what had been done.

What had been done was, from the general cultural vantage point, experimental, even revolutionary. But it was far easier to experiment in a utopia than in the pluralist, fluid society of the whole United States. For one thing, innovations are not difficult to introduce when a new world is beginning. For another, there was generally a community philosophy to which everyone purportedly subscribed, and the schools could be projected in accord with widely shared ends. Everyone took an interest, therefore; everyone played a part; even the children (at the start, at least) seemed to believe.

The choice of Pestalozzianism was integrally related to the political creed that shaped New Harmony. Pestalozzi was a Swiss who had elaborated on insights found in Jean-Jacques Rousseau's *Émile* and developed a theory of teaching "according to nature" and at once for a moral end. His desire, he said, was to make men out of beggars; this became the motivation for Owen's "New System of Society." He would take the "dregs," he told the world, the degraded and ignorant, and he would create an atmosphere in which they could grow. He would make them happy—

"this is the whole of my system," he said. He would enlighten them and keep them busy; and before long they would all be "virtuous and educated," free and dignified men.

Owen spoke of managing "the art of instruction" so that people would enjoy it; this he learned from Pestalozzi. The Swiss had asked that "love" be expressed in his graded classrooms, where the children's age was to determine what was to be taught and how. Pestalozzi himself had started with youngsters orphaned during the Napoleonic Wars. As his Children's Home became better known, he took more and more poor children, usually giving them homes. By the end of the Napoleonic era, he was known in many parts of Europe for his object lessons, his teacher-training programs, his break with Old Regime formalism and artificiality.

Owen's effort to remake an entire population of individuals was unsuccessful. After three years, New Harmony broke up and the land was parceled out and sold. "Grumbling," laziness, discontent, and disagreements destroyed it, as they had destroyed so many colonies before. Some said it was the lack of organized religion; some said it was the "Declaration of Mental Independence," condemning private property and weakening marriage ties. Owen said it was "premature to unite a number of strangers not previously educated for that purpose, who should carry on extensive operations for their common interest, and live together as a common family." The reports on the schools of New Harmony, however, survived. No one was to attempt quite so elaborate a utopia again, but many would attempt the "art of instruction" practiced there, although for very different purposes. Within a decade, the common school reformers would be traveling to Prussia to see the Pestalozzian methods being used in a militaristic state. Adaptations would be made to district school conditions in the American society Owen had described as being in its own way inequitable and unfree.

Men continued moving out to found new commonwealths just as they continued moving out to the frontiers. Some, like Owen's, collapsed because of simple human intransigence, some because of ignorance on the part of those who planned or ruled. The New England Utopia, founded by the Unitarian minister George Ripley, at first seemed destined to escape the misfortunes which had befallen all the others. Ripley selected the most literal of names—Brook Farm—for a site a few miles from Boston, far from the rigors of the wilderness. Intended neither as an example for mankind nor as an experiment in making men out of beggars, the community was to be "a society of liberal, intelligent, and cultivated persons, whose relations with each other would permit a more wholesome and simple life than can be led amidst the pressure of our competitive institutions." Its purpose was to be a kind of communal effort in self-realization; it would nurture the perfectibility of the enlightened instead of attempting to redeem the world.

Many of the great names in Unitarianism and Transcendentalism were associated with Brook Farm from its beginnings in 1842 through the seven years of its life. Gentlemanly and communal, it served as a showcase for the high-minded and light-hearted existence the sophisticated believed forbidden by the business-structured *status quo*. But even among the sometime visitors were those who doubted its practicality. Margaret Fuller, who was editing the Transcendentalist newspaper *The Dial* when Brook Farm began, was convinced that, no matter how cultivated, "we are not ripe to reconstruct society yet." But she came often to take part in Conversations with visitors like Emerson, Brownson, Robert Owen, Elizabeth Peabody—and with Nathaniel Hawthorne, who lived there briefly and later wrote *The Blithedale Romance* out of the experience and the knowledge that it failed.

Margaret Fuller, who was to become Zenobia in the book, was a representative "bluestocking," a driven liberal and reformer, an enthusiastic teacher. Ironically for one who did not believe the human race was "ripe," she exhausted herself in causes like labor reform and women's rights. In 1846, while on a trip to Europe, she married the Marquis Ossoli and fought with him for Italian unity in the revolution of 1848. When it failed, they decided to return to America with their baby; all three were killed in a shipwreck off the Long Island shore.

The spirit and eccentricity of a Margaret Fuller were mirrored in many individuals who worked and talked and handled tools at Brook Farm. Emerson noted, however, that the overall life of the community did not flare with the excitement of the individuals. The experiment lacked, he said, what was required to make a person "nobly mad." The scheme was "arithmetic and comfort," he asserted, "a rage in our poverty and politics to live rich and gentlemanlike, an anchor to leeward against a change of weather. . . ."

Even so, the Brook Farm school was exemplary, as only a school in a selective and enlightened community could be. There were infant classes there, primary classes, and six years of college-preparatory work. An effort was made "to insure a more natural union between intellectual and manual labor . . . to combine the thinker and the worker"; this was reflected in the balanced curriculum and in everyone's assignment to manual work. A student, like an adult participant, could move from a philosophy seminar to plowing a field. Handicrafts were as much a part of his field of study as the classic languages. There were concerts, debates, lectures, dramatic productions, and Conversations to satisfy every taste.

Hawthorne wrote of the people there being disoriented, becoming childish in their close companionship, losing the sense of reality and context. With the ordinary distinctions avoided, private disagreements seemed to increase; and, as Hawthorne saw it, the "nervous sympathy" that united the community caused any trivial unpleasantness to spread immediately throughout the Farm. The great obstacle to utopian living had always been human perversity, but here it seemed that the frailties of human beings were displayed more blatantly and comically than before. There were people convinced that the "single person" remained as problematic as society at large. There were others who insisted that neither friendship nor utopian planning nor the fullest, purest self-reliance could remove the tragic flaws implicit in American life.

Among such skeptics was Orestes Brownson, once a Unitarian minister, then—for a brief moment—a Transcendentalist. Before coming to Boston, he had been a wanderer from state to state, a seeker after creeds and regenerating faiths. He had worked with the New York Workingman's party before the depression of 1837; then he had founded a Society for Christian Union and Progress in a Boston suburb to provide a moral education for workingmen. It was while performing his ministry there that he became interested in Transcendentalism. Although he entered some of the Conversations and spent time at Brook Farm, he found the Emersonian view of "the genuine self against the world" far too optimistic. He believed men had to struggle if they were to be saved.

In 1840, aided by George Bancroft, he established a Democratic periodical, the *Boston Quarterly Review*. Its tone was radical and Jacksonian, and Brownson was free to express his views as he chose. Having seen much of human cruelty as well as frailty, he wrote of a dimension of life few of his New England friends had ever seen:

> We know no sadder sight on earth than one of our factory villages presents [*sic*], when the bell at break of day, or at the hour of breakfast, or dinner, calls out its hundreds or thousands of operatives. We stand and look at these hardworking men and women hurrying in all directions, and ask ourselves, where go the proceeds of their labors? The man who employs them, and for whom they are toiling as so many slaves, is one of our city nabobs, reveling in luxury; or he is a member of our legislature, enacting laws to put money in his own pocket; or he is a member of Congress, contending for a high Tariff to tax the poor for the benefit of the rich; or in these times he is shedding crocodile tears

over the deplorable condition of the poor laborer, while he docks his wages twenty five per cent. . . .

Some of this was traditional Jacksonian hostility to industry. Some was the result of Brownson's own perception of the loss of community due to the rift between capital and labor, due also to the discrepancies between the appearances and the realities of institutional life. "Not a few of our churches rest on Mammon for their foundation. The basement is a trader's shop."

Brownson had little faith in common schools because he did not think they could serve a legitimately moral end unless they restored continuities with "what was fundamental in that which has preceded. . . ." The fundamental thing, he thought, was the "communion" associated with faith in a supernatural reality. For the Transcendentalists, communion was an affair of last things, to be achieved by those who attained identification with the Oversoul. For Brownson, after a while, it had to do with first things—with the traditions rooted in the past.

As he pondered further, the Middle Ages began to seem the source of the greatest human sustenance; and he thought that the insistent "newness" of America, the tendency to break entirely with the Old World, was the reason for its immorality. It seemed necessary to him to cement new ties to the ages; one way to do so was to convert to Catholicism, the bearer of the medieval past. He joined the Church, therefore, and began to say that only in conversion was there hope.

De Tocqueville, visitor from a hierarchic state, had already warned Americans of what Brownson learned to lament. He had said: ". . . not only does democracy make every man forget his ancestors . . . it hides his descendants and separates his contemporaries from him; it throws him back forever upon himself alone and threatens in the end to confine him entirely within the solitude of his own heart."

There were indeed many people who were moving onward and turning their backs on the past; and there were Rip Van Winkles too, yearning for the old days, appalled by the "delapidations of time." There would be, for years to come, men reaching out to the "territory ahead," and others holding to the familiar, to the village way of life. There would be yea-sayers, chanting possibility; and there would be preachers of orthodoxy, pointing to what was lost. There would be the temptation of the open sea and the leeward pull to shore; excessiveness would assert its nobility and moderation its security.

The schools, however, by their very nature, had to look both ways. Despite laments like Brownson's, they were committed to the transmission of heritage. Despite de Tocqueville, they had to address themselves to the "descendants," to initiate the coming generations into the world their fathers had made. "We teach our boys to be such men as we are," Emerson said; and it was sad, considering how small he thought men had become.

Only Bronson Alcott talked specifically about schoolroom teaching among those who conversed at the Transcendental Club. But when he spoke of what it was to teach in the world as it existed, he omitted the role and influence of the problematic culture. He had had painful experiences with society during his career, but he was convinced that, wherever it took place, education was a personal, inner affair. "Education," he once wrote in his *Journal*, "is that process by which thought is opened out of the soul, and associated with outward . . . things." The environment, whether human or physical, seemed to him nothing more than a resource for the soul. The important thing was to insure that children were given freedom to converse, to "mirror" their ideas in subject matter, to realize and express what each potentially was.

Born in Connecticut, Alcott had begun teaching in 1823, in a Connecticut district school. Calvinism still dominated the area; but, in spite of it, he attempted to innovate in his peculiarly romantic way. Like other classrooms of the day, his was ungraded. Facing eighty pupils of assorted age, he was expected to use the customary Spellers and the moralizing Readers and to keep order by waving a ferrule. With a look of well-meaning innocence, he ignored instructions and went about treating his students as if each were entirely good and potentially wise. He bought slates and desks with the $135 he was paid for the four month term, and the community soon began realizing that the children were enjoying his class. The town government dismissed him for his eccentricities; he was unable to find another post in the state.

In 1829, he spent several months conducting a Boston Infant School, intended to prepare youngsters, according to custom, for admission to the district reading and writing schools. He met William Russell, editor of the *Journal of Education*, who was trying out Pestalozzian techniques at his Roxbury seminary for girls. Through Russell he met other Pestalozzians; and, as he moved from school to school, he became familiar with Joseph Neef's "Sketch of a Plan and Method" and other accounts of Pestalozzi's work. While teaching in a Boston Sunday School, he met William Ellery Channing. He came to know Emerson just at the time he was leaving the Unitarian church.

Alcott embarked on his greatest adventure in 1834, when he opened the Temple School on Tremont Street. Like many of the private experimental schools that would follow his, Alcott's attracted students from families who were enlightened and well-to-do. He did not have to cope with a town school committee, nor did he have to confront the problem of making "beggars" into citizens—well-adjusted, well-trained American workingmen.

His assistant was Elizabeth Peabody, who had worked in Roxbury with Russell. She was a highly gifted young woman, one of whose sisters was to marry Nathaniel Hawthorne, the other Horace Mann. Elizabeth was to assist with *The Dial* for a while; and, in 1877, she was to establish the first Froebelian kindergarten in Boston. She and Alcott administered a school which was as homelike, warm, and tasteful in appearance as any modern private school.

Grouped according to age, the children were given individual instruction when they needed it; each moved at his own speed. Creative writing and drawing were offered, "Self-Analysis," and

"Reasonings on Conduct and Discipline." Free Conversation was used even in the teaching of traditional subjects. Every pupil was encouraged to explore his own soul.

Alcott believed that faith could be nurtured only in spontaneity, and he thought it necessary to encourage free interpretation of the Gospels by every child. The so-called Conversation on the Gospels began, logically enough, with the mystery of Christ's birth; the artless Alcott was surprised when his pupils' parents began to protest. Miss Peabody resigned in the face of brewing scandal. Alcott hurriedly published the record of what had been said in order to show how innocent it was, but his fellow teachers in Boston derided his effort to explain. In 1837, the depression provided the parents an excuse for withdrawing all but two of the students from the school. One was a Negro girl Alcott had refused to dismiss in the face of earlier community threats; the other was William Russell's son. For two more years Alcott taught them with his own daughters in his home.

Emerson called Alcott "one *very man*, through and through"; and when Alcott gave up teaching and came to Concord as a laborer, Emerson helped him as much as he could. Some of his "Orphic Sayings" were published in *The Dial*: "By reasoning the soul strives to recover her lost intuitions . . ."; "The sensible world is spirit in magnitude, outspread before the senses for their analysis . . ."; "—Yet Nature is not separate from me; she is mine alike with my body. . . ."

Receiving an inheritance in 1841, the Alcotts went to England to be hailed by English mystics and educators. Upon return, Alcott was persuaded by an English friend to begin a "Con-sociate Family" establishment at Fruitlands, or "New Eden." It was a small ascetic utopia, forcibly acquainting the Alcotts with vegetarianism, cold water, and hard physical work. Alcott's British partner soon defected, however, and the community dissolved, adding one more to what Louisa May Alcott was to call "Transcendental Wild Oats."

Bronson Alcott spent most of his remaining years conducting Conversations in parlors and meeting halls for a little pay. He continued to think of himself as a teacher as he sat with his largely female circles of conversationalists, drawing each person out, trying to move each soul to find expression in what was said. It was to take until the 1870s and his meeting with the St. Louis Hegelians (or the founding of the Concord School of Philosophy) for him to make an impress on the history of thought. He was in many ways, however, the archetype of romantic Transcendentalism—and, in his teaching, a William Blake type of innocent whose impulses happened to resemble those of some progressivists of a later and much different day.

Nevertheless, like the utopians and his fellow idealists, Alcott presented a challenge to the raucous and burgeoning society Americans had made. Like others who were innocent, mystical, or dissident, he disclosed dimensions of experience which could not yet be encompassed by the rhetoric of schools. There was the "single person" still to be accounted for, in his inwardness as well as his effectuality. There was the moral striving of fallible men, for whom mere compliance was too little, perfection far too much. And there was the trial of living in what Hawthorne would call the "critical vortex" without becoming dwarfed and without becoming estranged.

4

THE "BALANCE WHEEL" AND THE PUBLIC SCHOOL CAMPAIGNS

Hope is required of those who work for public schools—hope, a singleness of purpose, and the ability to persuade. Man and his society must be conceived in such a way that the value of perpetuation is assumed. And what is believed must be communicated to the communities concerned, made part of "conventional wisdom," an aspect of what is taken to be "real."

The schoolmen of the 1830s and 1840s were shaping an almost visible edifice of recommendations while their contemporaries were voicing doubt, dissent, or despair. Competing with those who imaged the culture as decadent and fractured, reformers like Horace Mann worked to impart an immediacy to their models of human nature and the human world. They interwove description with prescription. They seized upon aspirations and expectations. They kept repeating that fulfillment was contingent upon a tax-supported school.

Mann grounded his faith in the notion of human plasticity, and the possibilities revealed prevented him from quite losing hope. He rejected the idea of original sin—and the idea of innate divinity as well. He believed children to be capable of every sort of behavior, ranging from the monstrous to the sublime. All depended on the environment surrounding them and the way in which they were taught.

Challenging sweet innocence and the "moral sense" at once, he was intensely curious about the workings of the mind. The dominant psychology had long been that of sense empiricism as developed by John Locke; but there was a growing dissatisfac-

tion with the conception of mind as an empty slate and with the
view of the self as a mental substance imprisoned in the chamber
of the brain.

The Romantics had long since refused the image of man as a
mechanism, a microcosm of a mechanistic cosmos. They sought
a wider, more inclusive vision of a human consciousness that was
creative—of a being with spirit, feeling, and sensuality, as well as
an ideating mind. Their desire was in accord with the requirements of an age centered on the "common man." It matched the
desire of those who relied upon "natural wisdom" and of those
seeking a definition of "imagination" appropriate to a New World
literature. It connected with Horace Mann's preoccupations,
too, although it did not fully embody them. He was in agreement
with Locke's teaching that character training was the school's
main undertaking; but, because he had to be concerned with
more than Locke's young gentleman, he saw character training
differently and rejected Locke's view of an innate moral sense.
This brought him, too, into the ranks of those who were asking
for a more variable, differentiated picture of "man." It made him
receptive to any proposal that might suggest a way of effectuat-
ing what he had in mind for the school.

Curiosity, therefore, and the need for a rationale brought him
to the pseudo-science of phrenology and the teachings of George
Combe. Combe had arrived from Scotland in 1838 and begun
lecturing immediately on the "faculties" of the mind. Mann, it
happened, had read the same Combe's *The Constitution of Man*
while preparing himself for his work as Secretary, and it seemed
to him that the charts and the scientific-sounding explanations
provided evidence that morality could be taught.

Combe had said convincingly that his studies of the confor-
mation of the skull would contribute to the advance of American
civilization. Mapping the regions of the cranium, he could identify
the "organ" associated with each mental faculty, each propensity,
he said. Once identified, particular faculties could be developed
to the degree required; particular propensities could be encouraged or controlled. With such information at hand, the common

schools could easily accomplish with the mass of children what Robert Owen had failed to do in his Utopia—and what those with "dark" perceptions were saying could not (in the nature of things) conceivably be done.

Mann proceeded to talk to his audiences about deliberately cultivating the faculties of temperance, humility, and virtue. He was enabled to embark on discussions of health and physical education, since he could now demonstrate that all the appetites must be satisfied if children were to develop harmoniously and learn to do what was right. Having discovered from Combe that frustrations in some areas might lead to overdevelopment in others, he could speak, almost in Rousseauist language, of all-around education and the exercise of natural capacities. His object was to show the feasibility of preventing "anarchy and violence"—and to indicate that the excessiveness characteristic of Americans could be contained. All that was required was a school to encourage tendencies opposite those which led to destructive behavior and thereby to limit overdevelopment of any single region of the brain. Evil propensities might forever be eradicated if the school were properly supported. It might not be possible to teach abhorrence of inequities, but it would be possible to teach all children temperateness, propriety, and the virtues of living by the Rule.

More important than the theory of phrenology was the confidence it inspired and some of the practices to which it gave birth. Before long, the sense of both was feeding into the expanding construct that was becoming "public education" in the popular mind. The educators themselves could not have given such ideas general currency—except, perhaps, in New England with its distinctive educational past. Accomplices were needed, individuals of all types and persuasions. A consensus was needed, a consensus so widespread that it would function like a force of nature in the land.

This is why the adult-education movement called "The American Lyceum" and the local institutes and lecture groups that followed were so important to the development of the schools.

Founded in Massachusetts in the 1820s, the lyceum movement proliferated through the decade of the 1830s, at the end of which it declined. In town and county lyceums, in the Western Literary Institute, in conventions and seminars, talks were given, discussions held, assemblies conducted, Conversations carried on. People gathered in the thousands over the East and the Midwest, searching for what they thought of as self-improvement, linking it with success. Those in the Midwest (who welcomed the movement most warmly) seemed to need new color and excitement in their lives. They wanted vicarious involvement with the larger world, the world they had left; they ached for alleviation of barren life routines. And so they came to hear the great men of their own and other countries: artists, scientists, explorers, statesmen from across the ocean, scholars, theologians, intellectuals of every breed.

The movement was voluntary, but it rose like a groundswell. The objective was popular enlightenment—education in the broadest possible sense. Several lyceums conducted children's classes, but most of those who benefited were old and young adults. Inevitably, schools were discussed, sometimes schools in other lands, sometimes local institutions when people complained of their inadequacy. Efforts were made to improve the skills of teachers. Celebrated educational thinkers like William Russell were consulted—and, before the day of the lyceums ended, Horace Mann.

The early years of the decade were the years of workingmen's demands for free and equal schools. "Friends of education" began appearing in regional groups around the country. Surveys were made. Petitions were sent to political representatives; now and then a governor was prevailed upon to declare for tax-supported schools.

Because a regular lecture circuit was established, the news of school reform could be carried beyond the localities where the reforms had taken place; this in part accounts for the wide national influence soon to be exerted by such ideas as Horace Mann's. The changes in Massachusetts were discussed when enough surveys were made for people to realize that one third of America's children went to no schools at all. In small communities everywhere, citizens began meeting to ask what should be done to raise the level of literacy, to teach the population a rudimentary morality, to preserve public order, to improve existing skills.

Consuming as interest in the subject became, most people remained indifferent to talk of tax support and state control. Those on the frontier shared a common hostility to controls of any sort. In rural areas, the Bible and "figgers" seemed sufficient learning for a boy; and this scarcely required tax-supported schools, it was believed, when there were itinerant teachers everywhere and church or charity groups willing to help. Voluntary enlightenment was one thing, people said; taxes and petty officials were another. And the gulf widened once more between those who had struck out for themselves and the artisans or workingmen who had stayed home.

Most reformers thought it obvious that nothing could be accomplished without tax support and expanding state control. Carter, Mann, and the others who had visited schools knew well the inequalities that could exist within a single state. Those who came regularly to lyceum meetings were also learning that without some deliberate teacher training schools would be valueless.

The proponents of state control knew vaguely of the Prussian system and its successes, and they welcomed a report on Prussia when it was translated in 1835. It had been written by Victor Cousin, Minister of Instruction in the new French constitutional monarchy, who had been sent to observe the central administration in Prussia—and the Pestalozzian methods utilized in the schools. The lyceums discussed it as a model of what effective education ought to be; and, although some found in it ammunition for their attacks on centralization (and "tyranny"), the report gave additional substance to the consensus taking shape.

Feelings were so strong that one educator after another embarked on voyages to Europe to see the Prussian schools for themselves. Among the first was Henry Barnard, who remained abroad from 1835 to 1837 and who was made a member of the newly established Connecticut State Board on his return. Afterwards he became Secretary and worked for four years to overcome a blank popular indifference to the Connecticut district schools. In 1838, more than half the children in the state did not attend school although private schools were flourishing for the children of the propertied; the teachers were more inexperienced and inept than the Massachusetts teachers observed by Horace Mann. With a determination almost as firm as Mann's, but with less of the prophet about him and more of the businessman, Barnard succeeded in arousing some of the citizens of Connecticut to pay attention to their publicly supported schools. He began a teachers' institute in the spirit of what he had seen abroad, worked on problems of school construction, attempted to establish libraries, and began a Connecticut journal similar to Mann's in Massachusetts. In 1824, the governor of the state charged him with unnecessary expenses and succeeded in abolishing the State Board, and with it the Secretaryship. Barnard went on to Rhode Island to battle for the cause among resistant, apathetic farm-owners, only to return to Connecticut in the 1850s as principal of the state normal school.

In the meantime, others were making the pilgrimage to Europe on behalf of their state legislatures, or, in the case of Alexander Bache, on behalf of a college board of trustees. Calvin B. Stowe, who had been schooled in Massachusetts, was sent by the legislature of Ohio to study, particularly, the Prussian teachers' seminaries, established by Pestalozzians. Ohio, with its population of New Englanders, passed a state law calling for tax-supported schools in 1838; but it would not be until 1853 that the schools established would be free. Stowe's reports, however, became influential, as were Caleb Mills' in lagging, half-illiterate Indiana and those of Calvin Wiley in North Carolina, the only Southern state to establish common schools.

Having read the reports of those who had visited the Prussian schools, Horace Mann set off in 1843. He studied the school systems in seven European countries and summed up his findings in his seventh Annual Report. There, pointing to the stiffness and inefficiency of Massachusetts classrooms, he described the "beautiful relation of harmony and affection" between teachers and students abroad, and the "sweet and humanizing influences" which seemed to prevail in the Pestalozzian schools. His description aroused the anger of thirty-one Boston schoolmasters, who saw in the Report a direct attack on the Massachusetts schools. They issued a lengthy public statement which took Mann to task for proposing a slackening of discipline, oral instruction instead of textbook study, and the "word method" of introducing children to reading instead of the letter method which prevailed. Mann responded at even greater length; there was a rejoinder, then another answer from Mann. The controversy was widely discussed and publicized; and, because of it, the news of European reforms penetrated wherever there were newspapers and magazines.

The new methods were not to be adopted in any meaningful way until the Civil War, even in the Massachusetts schools. Mann and his co-workers had promoted normal schools successfully, doubled the salaries of many teachers, and raised the requirements for certification. The district boards were releasing their hold on some of the schools; state supervision was increasing; local tax support was becoming widespread. Nevertheless the system was not yet ready to accept the reforms being instituted in classrooms abroad. The teachers who learned of them said they were nothing but (as the schoolmasters had put it) "hotbed theories." Still held responsible for hundreds of children in ungraded rooms, the experienced and hardworking Master or Schoolma'am saw no alternative to rote learning, oral recitations, and the use of the ferrule.

The "one-room schoolhouse" of American tradition is generally thought of in a village context; and the single teacher (usually female) is thought of as having been eminently well qualified to handle her group of youngsters, no matter what the spread in age. Even when the effects of nostalgia are discounted, the situation in the little red village schoolhouse must have been far superior to that in the enormous city schools. Until the late 1840s, they too were organized as one- and two-room schools.

In most urban districts, there were large reading and writing sections, often on different floors. It was not unusual for each section to hold as many as two hundred children and for three teachers to be held responsible for the entire school. Most children had had to attend infant or primary schools before being admitted to the reading and writing schools, but by the end of the 1830s this requirement was being altered, and upper and lower reading sections were organized within some district schools. Spelling (in Webster's blue-backed Speller) and word-calling were conducted as "reading"; arithmetic was taught with penmanship in "writing" class. Here and there, as more and more nonreaders entered, the upper and lower sections subdivided into classes divided roughly according to ability or age.

Even so, the teachers continued to face twenty or thirty rows of children in the Boston and Quincy schools, and wherever else people settled near factories or in slums. The teacher rarely had more than two years of training beyond his own reading-school education; and he was scarcely equipped to do more than hear recitations in the vast classes to which he was assigned. Pupils were drilled endlessly, therefore; they were promoted on the basis of proficiency in memorization. More often than not, those who survived past the age of eleven without dropping out were those who memorized even their arithmetic texts.

Examinations were prepared by town school committees composed of prominent citizens, all laymen. In a real sense, therefore, everything taught was predetermined by the community outside the school—by local selectmen, textbook publishers (whose numbers increased each year), and sometimes by the large taxpayers or the spokesmen for the neighborhood church. Failures were common. The examining committees of many towns lamented the poor showing, the technical errors, the lack of information, the inability to understand words pronounced in the course of oral reading.

In his 1845 Report, Mann wrote at length about the contribution made by the Boston school committees who had replaced the traditional oral tests with written examinations. The system was far more impartial, he said, fairer, and more reliable. Even so, until the 1850s, most town committees continued to stress declamation, word-calling, letter recognition, and penmanship. This tended to confirm teachers in routine, "memoriter" practices like hearing recitations.

Mann himself had said categorically that this was "not teaching." As he saw it, teaching involved "the exposition of the principle contained in the book; showing its connection with life, with action, with duty; making it the nucleus around which to gather all related facts and . . . principles:—it is this, and this only, which can be appropriately called teaching." But the quality of teaching was integrally related to evaluation practices and to the methods teachers had learned to use; and these were largely dependent on the opportunity to grade children according to aptitude and age. Without some mode of grading, it was impossible to structure lessons for specific classes. There could be little thought about adjusting instruction to stages of growth, little thought about relating "principle" to the lives and duties of particular children. All was left to the textbook publisher, whose collections of facts and rules (privately digested among the crowded ranks of children) could be learned by rote.

The districts were slow to follow the Pestalozzian example; but in 1846 John Philbrick, the Quincy Superintendent of Schools, reorganized the grammar school in his community to accommodate its eight hundred pupils in twelve classrooms instead of in the usual two or three divisions. Three years later, he reorganized the lower schools in the same way. Other Superintendents might have done the same more rapidly than they did had it not been for an unexpected influx of Irish immigrants, which taxed all facilities and made reforms even harder to effect.

The historic famine of 1847, however, had sent thousands of hungry Irish people fleeing for their lives. In Boston alone, more than thirty thousand victims of British neglect landed in the first few months after the hunger began. Many were beggars; hundreds were sick; thousands were infants struggling to survive. They found refuge in the cellars of the city or in the rundown mansions of Ward 8, now reconverted into a hill of appalling tenements, shacks, and sheds. Children began appearing daily on the city's main streets. They were in search of food and money and sometimes jobs to do. The city fathers began warning against the "moral cesspool" being created, the seeping depravity and crime. The Catholic Church, overwhelmed, could not provide; and, little by little, some of the Irish children began appearing in the district schools.

With heterogeneity heightened even more, with an intensified threat to public peace being everywhere defined, there were more demands than ever before that something be done about the schools. Ironically, the panacea which came first to mind was another series of textbooks, already in use in communities throughout the United States. They were the first and second *Eclectic Readers*, first published by William Holmes McGuffey in 1836. They were to become the foundation of a series of graded readers which would be used by four generations of Americans; and, to compound the irony of their adoption in Boston, they represented one of the first adaptations of Pestalozzian principles to teaching in the schools.

McGuffey and his son, attempting to adjust each lesson to a particular mental age, had the cultivation of "pure moral and religious sentiment" in mind—the traditional enterprise of character training, or making children "good." Using Pestalozzi's object-lesson approach, they grounded the course in immediate experience by using an initial-picture alphabet, with each letter linked to some ordinary object—an axe, a cat, a dog, a house, a school. For all its orientation to the practical, however, the textbook's spirit was similar to that of the old *New England Primer*.

There was good reason for this; since the *Readers* originated in Ohio, where most people were familiar with the *Primer* alphabet, from Adam's Fall to Zaccheus who "Did climb the Tree, Our Lord to see." McGuffey had become acquainted with Calvin Stowe at the Western Literary Institute, and their conversations had led to a contract with a Cincinnati publisher. McGuffey was asked to do a series that would bring light ("from above," McGuffey said) to the thousands of recently arrived children entering the public schools.

Ohio was like a reproduction of early eighteenth-century New England. The inhabitants were frequently like William Holmes McGuffey, with memories of painful, brave migrations, hard work, and success won through years of unassisted effort under the unsmiling eyes of God. They were closer to the wilderness, even in 1836, then a Mann or Barnard ever was. McGuffey had been an itinerant teacher, hiking from town to town through wilderness and woods. He demonstrated a strong desire to create a morality that would stave off the wilderness—a morality like an old-fashioned stockade. In an introduction to one of the *Fifth Readers*, the author wrote that "new concepts" were more dangerous than old prejudices. "The novelty of an opinion in any moral question is a presumption against it." The views transmitted were given the absoluteness of the catechism; and the *Readers* built a hundred bridges between the Puritan past and the children of the unregenerate present, who were told they could only be American if they learned what was True.

Pestalozzi had always stressed natural development and "free activity"; yet the McGuffeys put his method effectively to work for what was actually an opposite goal. But as we have seen, only a Transcendentalist or a utopian in those days could put his trust in spontaneity. Those who assented to Trade and Manifest Destiny were those who believed in character training as discipline, in knowledge as the power to control. A Bronson Alcott—like a Robert Owen—could not make himself heard by those subjecting a continent to their will while a McGuffey (and a Mann) spoke a language familiar to thousands because it echoed the past and made virtues useful in the present appear derivations of the virtues which had once made men "elect."

Not surprisingly, Pestalozzianism was reinterpreted, just as Jeffersonianism had been. The *Readers* carefully conducted children up a ladder of preachments and stories, with pictures at in-

tervals, lists of words to be spelled, sounded, and in time understood. They guided children, level by level, around and around a
circle of virtues: promptness, goodness, kindness, honesty, truth-
fulness, piety. Generations were warned against debt, encouraged in industriousness, promised that effort would blossom in
reward, that vice would be punished—that everyone would get
what he deserved. As age groups were organized into classes and
didactic questioning became a kind of public undertaking, with
many children listening or taking part, it was as if there were a
concerted public campaign to woo youngsters into mastery of
good habits—into thrift, ambition, and self-discipline—as they
were being inducted into the American way.

With the help of McGuffey *Readers* and similar ones, the
common school found an answer to the strains of duality and the
awareness of human fallibility. By 1850, a start toward free-
school organization had been made in every Northern state. In
the East and Midwest, almost a quarter of the white school-age
population was reported to be in attendance at public schools.
Because the country was still expanding, because it was raw and
new in so many areas, the youngsters coming out of schools
found the world rich in opportunities, many of them unknown to
older generations. As in the days of the earliest settlements, dis-
continuities appeared between the life experiences of fathers
and sons. The "wisdom" of the elders became frequently irrelevant; and, as de Tocqueville had foreseen, familiar traditions
could no longer sustain.

The school, insufficient though it might have been, stepped
into the breach for many and at least provided a moral framework, a set of authoritative controls. Something like the "social
principle" proposed by Mann became the source of a conscience
for many young men set loose in the open, competitive world.
Even in the mining camps and railroad settlements there were
those who remained in some sense "genteel." And those who
were excessive in acquisitiveness were frequently likely to com-
pensate by cultivating intense respectability in domestic life, by
engaging in philanthropy, by becoming pillars of the church. It

seemed far more important, in the end, to build a solid, gabled house on Main Street than to be known as a buccaneer—more important to be a leading citizen than an adventurer.

"Let us affront and reprimand the smooth mediocrity and squalid contentment of the times, and hurl in the face of custom, and trade and office, the fact which is the upshot of all history, that there is a great responsible Thinker and Actor working wherever a man works. . . ." That was Emerson, still demanding that the docile ones assert themselves, take personal risks, break free.

And the answer? Some pointed to the equalities achieved, the community attained. Some only stared uncomprehendingly while voices murmured around them; and the words from the old *Primer* returned:

> *In Adam's Fall*
> *We sinned All.*

5

NATHANIEL HAWTHORNE'S "PEEP-HOLE" VIEW

In 1836, in his darkened room in Salem, Nathaniel Hawthorne wrote a fable called "The Maypole of Merry Mount." The focal images in the tale are a maypole and a whipping post, each the "banner staff" of a distinctive settlement in colonial New England.

The action begins with a sunset scene, when the inhabitants of Merry Mount are gathering around the beribboned, wreathed, and painted pine tree for a dance. They are dressed as for a Dionysian revel: some wear animal heads or limbs; some wear fool's caps, others fur and silks and rags. One is masquerading as an English priest, "decked with flowers, in heathen fashion" and with vine leaves on his head. The occasion is the wedding of the Lord and Lady of the May.

The Lady is sad amid the gaiety, although she knows that sadness is not allowed. Soon the young Lord feels his own "dreary presentiment of inevitable change." A band of armored Puritans—"iron men"—come through the woods from the neighboring colony. They are led by Governor Endicott and they have come to "establish their jurisdiction over the gay sinners," to make New England "a land of clouded visages, of hard toil, of sermon and psalm forever."

Endicott cuts down the maypole with his sword; the revelers are captured and sentenced to punishment. Only the Lord and Lady arouse the Governor's pity; they are given proper Puritan clothing to wear and offered an opportunity to repent.

And Endicott, the severest Puritan of all who laid the rock foundation of New England, lifted the wreath of roses from the ruin of the Maypole and threw it, with his own gauntleted hand, over the heads of the Lord and Lady of the May. It was a deed of prophecy. As the moral gloom of the world overpowers all systematic gayety, even so was their home of wild mirth made desolate amid the sad forest. They returned to it no more. But as their flowery garland was wreathed of the brightest roses that had grown there, so, in the tie that united them, were intertwined all the purest and best of their earthly joys. They went heavenward, supporting each other along the difficult path which it was their lot to tread, and never wasted one regretful thought on the vanities of Merry Mount.

So, as Hawthorne told it, civilization was imposed upon the wilderness. The "jurisdiction" established may be felt to be the beginning of adulthood by those concerned with children and with schools. When the Governor throws the wreath, he may be officiating at a rite of passage, an initiation into the world of serious things.

Whether the gaieties of Merry Mount are associated with Cavaliers, with wilderness, or with Adamic innocence, the "iron men" are not only Puritans, but also carriers of the rule of Right, the "moral gloom" of the world. Like teachers, they are committed to inducting the tractable into the dominant way of life and disciplining the intractable until they learn to conform. They do their work solemnly, almost kindly, like agents of Necessity. Loss is suffered; but the process of acculturation into the Puritan world is accepted as a kind of gift. Dancing and feasting are now recognized as "vanities." The only thing worth salvaging from the past is love.

In this tale, there is no either–or: innocence and experience are both ambiguous; neither settlement is wholly adequate from the human point of view. Nevertheless, an organized community life is shown to be a necessity, since man needs more than spontaneity and freedom if he is to grow. Hawthorne was neither an Emerson nor a Mann. He did not believe in building barriers against what Mann called "anarchy."

When he wrote the story of Merry Mount, Hawthorne was concerned above all with entering into the life he saw from his window in Salem. He had been in retreat for almost a decade, trying to learn how to see the world, trying to remove himself from his own dark wood. Below his window pulsed the life of a seaport town, hectic with the activity of merchantmen and sailing ships. The days of small-sized ports were numbered; but Salem was still exporting raw materials to Europe and unloading coffee, sugar, tea, and manufactured goods on the cobbled quays. Empty freighters were bringing immigrants from England, Scotland, Wales. The Customs House, where Hawthorne himself would one day work, still held piles of goods in its fastnesses and pulsed with the affairs of men like the Peter Goldthwaite he would one day describe—with "just the sort of capital for building castles in the air."

Hawthorne lived apart, an outsider and a solitary. His separation has been attributed to melancholy, delicacy, and to a privateness that alienated him from philistines and robust seekers after success. But this is only one side of it; his withdrawal anticipated a tendency that would become evident in the lives of many artists in Europe as well as America. It was related to the rise of industry, the expansion of cities, the development of a middle-class reading public; it involved rejections of traditional certainties, the religious virtues, sanctions of many kinds. Men like Edgar Allan Poe suffered it; so did Charles Baudelaire, Gustave Flaubert, Fyodor Dostoievski, Stephen Crane, Mark Twain, and many others.

Hawthorne, living through the pioneering and tension of the Jacksonian and post-Jacksonian years, moved through the experience of alienation and beyond it, but the condition remained significant in its effect on his work. His irony and sense of doubleness may be attributed to it. Even when he met Sophia Peabody in 1838, when "the world found me out in my lonely chamber and called me forth," the outsider's vantage point continued to be the one from which he peered. His engagement and marriage healed him considerably, but the habit of looking through peepholes and mirrors remained.

This meant a fictional world viewed in oblique perspective many times, revealing things ordinarily unseen. Involvement with other men helped him to form what was revealed but did not alter his peculiar view. On occasion, he would try to alter it, as when he attempted to make a home for himself and Sophia at Brook Farm; but his mind was too mordant for him to put his faith in a Utopia, and he did not stay as long as a year.

Millennium seemed impossible because of what he saw of human nature. The only redemption he could imagine was that which men might attain through knowledge of themselves—and measurement of their condition against the ultimate. Like Mann, he had been reared in Calvinism and trained to think of what lay secreted within each person as well as what lay inscrutably beyond. He would not agree with Emerson that "disagreeable appearances, swine, spiders, snakes, pests, mad-houses, prisons, enemies, vanish," once the higher law is seen, and "you conform your life to the pure idea in your mind."

Hawthorne perceived darkness and light, as the schoolmen did; but for him the poles were the black of a Massachusetts night and a red that burned. In his created universe there were no final solutions, but always a danger of inundation. It was part of the nature of things that shadows could always fall. He knew that the orders men made for themselves were tenuous and to some extent insufficient, no matter how acclaimed. There could be no *stasis* in America, no perfection; there were no guarantees.

No measure of enlightenment, then, no "voluntary compliance" would keep forbidden wishes from festering; nothing could finally tear away the veil, remove the serpent, heal the "haunted mind." In the parable "Earth's Holocaust," human beings try to make a new beginning in perfect lightness and clarity. Like utopians, they attempt to rid themselves of shibboleths and the "wornout trumpery" that have kept them from living according to Nature and her benevolent law. A great bonfire is lit on the prairie, and people come from far distances to throw in what they can no longer use. They burn armor, medals, crowns, scepters, all the badges of a dead European past. They go on to destroy liquor, coffee, weapons, implements of torture, and at length, law codes, the gallows, the Scriptures, and the accouterments of religion, libraries of "dead men's thought."

They are preparing for a return to innocence, for a new era of beneficence and peace, when neither laws nor prisons nor currency will be needed anymore. Everyone is to live according to natural reason alone, at "a stage of progress . . . far beyond what the wisest and wittiest men of former ages had ever dreamed. . . ." But the dream of return to eighteenth-century cities of light is destroyed by what Herman Melville was to call "the power of blackness" that always worked through Hawthorne's art. A stranger appears, listening to the last hangman lamenting with the last thief and the last murderer that there "will be no world for us any longer." The stranger—"dark-visaged"—reassures them and tells them they will see good days yet. "There's one thing that these wiseacres have forgotten to throw into the fire, and without which all the rest of the conflagration is just nothing at all; yes, though they had burned the earth itself to a cinder." When asked what has been forgotten, he says, "the human heart. . . . And unless they hit upon some method of purifying that foul cavern, forth from it will reissue all the shapes of wrong and misery. . . ."

These shapes, for Hawthorne, are what haunt the mind. They are the vestiges of original desires which, under the masks of civilization, show themselves as sins. They are sins because, if they are not so named, men cannot live together according to man-made, arbitrary laws. Rooted as they are in a common past, the desires which are sinful are ineradicable; and human beings have to suffer with them, disguise them, strive to resist them as long as life goes on. No one is spared. No reform, no revolution can alter man's moral nature; no utopian renovation can diminish the strain imposed by the community's demand.

To affirm this may be to deny the American Dream and to

challenge the claims of a school. But to refuse to believe it is to expose oneself to a shock of despair like the one which afflicts the hero of "Young Goodman Brown." Brown is an ordinary citizen of colonial Salem who has been tempted by the devil to attend a suspect gathering in the woods at night. When he discovers all the pious townspeople he knows taking part in the forbidden ritual, he is horrified; and when he sees the pink ribbon of Faith, his wife, he loses all hope and faith. He is alienated not by "the stain of guilt" that marks his fellow citizens but by the human condition itself. He does not know that he is sharing in the "communion" of his race by worshiping at the devil's altar; nor does he understand that the sense of sin is part of the human heritage, making men equal under the sky.

The communion spoken of by the Transcendentalists is here transvalued. It refers to men's beginnings now, not to their spiritual goal. And the passions which have been thought disintegrative are seen to be the ones that bind. Goodman Brown isolates himself in scorn and bitterness at what he has perceived about man. In "The Minister's Black Veil," Father Hooper does the same by wearing a veil over his face as "a type and a symbol" of the darkness resident in every human being. The veil repels his parishioners instead of enlightening them; it alienates the woman he is to marry; it makes him see everything in half-light, darkened by the veil. Goodman Brown's situation is the reverse, but the meaning is the same. The townspeople in "The Minister's Black Veil" refuse to confront the fact that each has something to hide. The minister dies in his egotism, still refusing to remove the cloth and show his kinship with ordinary men.

For Hawthorne, sensed experience is often an affair of symbols—in Emerson's language, a "veil." In "Rappaccini's Daughter" a beautiful girl and a garden full of flowers are delusive in their freshness: the scientist, Dr. Rappaccini, has made them deadly with experimental poison. The student, Giovanni, trying to take "a more rational view" of life, finds in the flowers "a symbolic language to keep him in communion with Nature" and, refusing to believe that a father would experiment on his own daughter, pursues Beatrice in spite of what he hears. The Emersonian vision seems to be reversed, since beauty is now a veil for destructiveness and death. Giovanni at length calls Beatrice "a poisonous thing"; but, in truth, she is spiritually pure, innocently in search of love. Again the tables turn. One cannot believe one's eyes.

Knowledge itself may be suspect in Hawthorne's universe, particularly the knowledge used to exert power over man. In "The Birthmark," Aylmer is a man of science in the days "when the comparatively recent discovery of electricity and other kindred mysteries of Nature seemed to open paths into the region of miracle." Insatiable in his quest for knowledge, he decides to experiment on his wife and to remove the birthmark which is her single flaw. Aylmer has been striving after supernatural knowledge. He has believed that he "redeemed himself from materialism by his strong and eager aspiration towards the infinite." His wife dies when the birthmark disappears, because it was the single sign of her mortality, the thing that bound her to the earth. Aylmer's earthiness, on the other hand, has prevented him from uncovering the ultimate. A representative overreacher, he is destroyed by his human blindness, by ordinary human fallibility.

The Faustian theme is further explored in "Ethan Brand," the tale of the Berkshire mountain lime-burner who ascends heights of wisdom unattainable by "the philosophers of the earth, laden with the lore of universities." He is said to have launched his quest in "sympathy for mankind" and a desire to find the "Unpardonable Sin." He, too, has sought a knowledge forbidden to fallible men; in seeking it, he has experimented on or manipulated other human beings, thus committing the very sin he sought to understand and overcome.

Because Ethan Brand has used his wisdom for illicit ends, and because the "star-lit eminence" of knowledge he attained has isolated him from other men, he has lost hold of "the magnetic chain of humanity." He has forgotten that he is a "brother-man." Loneliness and isolation have "disturbed the counterpoise between his mind and heart"; and he has become an exemplar of the self-reliance De Tocqueville called "disintegrative"—a wholly self-sufficient man with a heart of stone.

His story culminates in an oblique demand for wholeness, for the restoration of "counterpoise." This equilibrium is akin to the "inner checks" Horace Mann recommended when he contemplated abnormality and excess. Moral training, as Mann saw it, would make it possible to cultivate opposing tendencies in such a person as Ethan Brand—humility perhaps, or temperance, or piety. Once equilibrium was re-established in such a fashion, instruction in righteousness was likely to succeed.

Hawthorne, however, saw strange disguises and haunted minds when he looked at men, and he had little faith that humanity could be perfected in the world that had come to be. In his tale "The Celestial Railroad," the narrator dreams of a modern pilgrimage to what was once John Bunyan's Celestial City. Instead of traveling on foot as Bunyan's Christian did, the pilgrims now proceed by train and ferryboat. Mechanical invention has removed the obstacles which Christian had to labor over: there is a bridge over the Valley of Humiliation, and gaslight illuminates the Valley of the Shadow of Death. The traveler's guide at length turns out to be the devil himself, but his name has been changed to "Mr. Smooth-it-away."

Hawthorne, saying it this way, pointed to the hypocrisies and equivocations accompanying the increasing ease of daily life. What Mann described as "moral compliance" became nothing more than automatic, outward conformity in the artist's illusioned world. Men, he thought, were becoming numb to ambiguities and inhumanity, undisturbed even by sin. Yet they were constantly being tempted in America, endangered by estrangement if not by sin itself. They were being drawn into unheard-of quests by the high courage and autonomy that had sent them originally in pursuit of a Dream.

Like Orestes Brownson, then, Hawthorne wrote of the need for community and attempted to weave continuities with the far-off past. It was not that he opposed the forward movement in the land, nor that he believed in a return. It was, rather, that he saw

men of the past as conscious of their predicament as human beings. He saw, especially when he looked back to colonial America, lives lived with a sense of momentousness in the effort to
appear "elect" in the eyes of a silent God. Compared with the
flatland of the Age of Trade, the earlier age seemed to him to be
an eminence, and this in spite of bigotries, witchburnings, orthodoxies. As an artist, therefore, he moved back to it in search of
illumination for the present. And, moving back, he found fore-
shadowings of a future he himself did not yet know—images of
fulfillment unexplored even in the age through which he lived.

Hawthorne wrote *The Scarlet Letter* in 1850, when he had
been married to Sophia for eight years. During those years he
had been appointed to the Customs House for the second time
and worked there as a surveyor from 1846 to 1849, while the
Mexican War was going on. When the Whigs returned to power,
he knew he would be discharged; by the time dismissal came, he
was already launched on a three-year period of novel-writing and
his most consistent productivity. The Customs House, with its
precipitates from the past, was, he said, the source of *The Scarlet Letter*; for it was there that he came upon the emblem in the
shape of a red *A* and there that he came to terms with his "own
reality."

The novel begins with an ironic rendering of colonial Boston,
another settlement centered on a whipping post. "The founders
of a new colony," Hawthorne wrote, "whatever Utopia of human
virtue and happiness they might originally project, have invari-
ably recognized it among their earliest practical necessities to al-
lot a portion of the virgin soil as a cemetery, and another portion
as the site of a prison." There is one semblance of purity: the wild
rosebush at the doorway of the prison, which may represent
compassion, wilderness, or "some sweet moral blossom" for the
reader's hand.

Although the population of the colony seems coarse and
heartless, the community is not presented as evil. Hawthorne
had repeatedly made it clear that he thought communion a necessity, that isolation could freeze a personality, that egotism

could destroy. Here he had chosen to explore what it was like to be a free, exceptional individual who knew enough not to break the "magnetic chain."

The central theme is sin and the range of attitudes provoked by its existence; but there is a pervasive ambiguity which makes sin and evil both seem to be the appearances of what occurs within human beings when they become "civilized." The worst of the sinners is Roger Chillingworth, perhaps the most civilized of all the characters. A scholar of the type of Dr. Rappaccini, he has just emerged from the wilderness when the action begins. He stands "in a strange disarray of civilized and savage costume" to watch the adulteress and her child on the scaffold of the pillory. Hester Prynne recognizes him from the high platform because he cannot hide his deformity or the "bleared optics" in his scholarly face. He is a scientist, "skilled in physic," and with the ability to "read the human soul." It is this that makes him a "fiend" when, like Ethan Brand, he uses his genius to degrade and injure a fellow man.

More pathetic and less dignified is Arthur Dimmesdale, on which sin acts as if it were an infected wound. This is because he is keeping it secret, refusing to testify that he is an adulterer even though his congregation looks upon him as a saintly minister. Rendered pallid and therefore spiritual in appearance, he wears a disguise, a mask like Father Hooper's, until the moment of his death; and even then the townspeople refuse to see. Their insistent reverence is a type of wish-fulfillment; but, deceiving them, Dimmesdale is isolated in his pain. If it were not for the deception, he would be an ordinary, pedantic minister, too weak to stir his audiences, too innocent to inspire. If Chillingworth had not tormented him so effectively, he might eventually have confessed and moved away. He is too frail a character to be transfigured by his sin.

In this fictional universe, growth and virtue are both functions of uncommon strength. Hester Prynne suggests what may be an ideal of full humanity: the person strong enough to admit desire and to acknowledge fallibility. In a world of insensitive, conforming creatures, she is powerful, passionate, reminiscent of pagan goddesses and the "Divine Maternity." If she were not so warm and so responsive, she would not have committed adultery with its risk of pregnancy and shame. Avoiding temptation, she would have escaped punishment; but she might then have remained the passive young Englishwoman who had married an elderly man of "the study and the cloister," shut against the claims of life.

That man, Chillingworth, had disappeared on his voyage to America. If he had not, and if Hester had not come alone, she would not have fallen at all. But then she would not have grown into nobility and freedom, nor become the town's scapegoat, Samaritan, and, at long last, its saint. Her fall turns out to have been a "fortunate fall." Without it, she would not have seized the opportunity to probe and choose; she would not have been redeemed.

Biblical overtones multiply as the story proceeds; but Hester's realization is achieved in a secular frame, within a Puritan community which tortures and ostracizes those who offend. She accepts the primitive punishment as a deserved ignominy. Nevertheless, as she tells Dimmesdale, "What we did had a consecration of its own. We felt it so! We said so to each other!" They are in the woods when she says that, seven years after their love affair. It is only in the impinging wilderness of woods that natural consecrations can be affirmed. The society must impose its laws in the settled places, and here exceptions cannot be made. Hester acknowledges this where natural consecrations are concerned; and, although she has always been free to depart, she chooses to stay and accede to punishment to live outside the village limits and to wear a scarlet A. The fact that her lover is in Boston has much to do with her decision; more significant is her belief that she would be choosing an anonymity, a meaninglessness if she left. Human lives gain their color, Hawthorne wrote, from the great events that occur in their course; and people hesitate to leave the places where they have experienced great pain or joy.

They are "the more irresistible, the darker the tinge," he said. "Her sin, her ignominy were the roots she had struck into the soil."

This was Hawthorne's response to what Emerson saw as the mediocrity and what he himself felt as the numbness, the hypocrisy of the age in which they lived. It was his response to the yea-saying of those who believed they could teach young people "self-control," to the aspirations of those who thought that, given the proper environment, they could insure the self-perfecting of every living man. Whether the objective was to build barriers against immorality or to prevent its growth through reform, the tendency was to talk as if the good life and the good society should exclude blackness and reject the possibility of sin.

Not only did this threaten human beings; it made confrontation of hidden things somehow unthinkable. Denial was the inevitable consequence, and with denial went inauthenticity, what Sören Kierkegaard was even then calling "untruth." If citizenship and virtue were to demand a kind of godliness, the myth of perfectibility might be fed—but the "reality" of the single person would be thrust underground and would fester there.

Hawthorne's Hester Prynne enacts a scornful challenge to such an either–or. Sinful and heroic as she is, she can neither abrogate, withdraw, nor deny. She lives on the outskirts of the town, on a curving peninsula at the edge of the sea, and her cottage faces the western wilderness. She discovers a strange liberation through her ostracism and engages in "a freedom of speculation"; she wanders "without a clew in the dark labyrinth of mind." She finds no radiance of transcendental insight; and no doors open to a sustaining Oversoul. She learns enough to be critical and to cope with mystery. She looks from her "estranged point of view at human institutions, and whatever priests or legislators had established; criticizing all with hardly more reverence than the Indian would feel for the clerical band, the judicial robe, the pillory, the gallows, the fireside, or the church."

Set free, she becomes a stranger; but she voluntarily moves into the community each day. She performs services having to do with birth, death, and the ceremonial occasions of Puritan life.

Still feminine and passionate, she needs to commune with other human beings; and, as time passes, she begins to be recognized, accepted, even loved. She is the one who helps when help is most deeply needed, and she can understand what others are afraid to name.

Barred from normal undertakings, she expresses some of her feeling and energy in the artistic handiwork she does. She ornaments linens, cloaks, and shrouds, sewing in red and gold on the gray surfaces of the world. Her "nymph child" is dressed as if she were a living work of art, an emblem of the wild and beautiful, of maypoles and outlawed delights.

The child is a sign of Hester's refusal to resign herself. Yet little Pearl refuses to go to her mother when Hester, during her single meeting with Dimmesdale, takes off her formal Puritan cap and lets her hair fall over her shoulders, "dark and rich, with at once a shadow and a light in its abundance. . . ." Like that cap and the embroidered A on her dress, the controls of civilization are made to appear for the moment illusory, codes people somehow agree to maintain. Ironically, however, Hester has defined herself as mother and as personality *within* the moral institutions of the community. Her child will not recognize her in the guise of a creature of the woods.

Even so, where the community is concerned, Pearl herself is as much outsider as her mother; Hawthorne specifically challenged prevailing modes of child upbringing when he described the Boston children who show contempt for Pearl:

> . . . the children of the settlement, on the grassy margin of the street, or at the domestic thresholds, disporting themselves in such grim fashion as the Puritanic nurture would permit; playing at going to church, perchance; or at scourging Quakers; or taking scalps in a sham-fight with the Indians; or scaring one another with freaks of imitative witchcraft.

Pearl is "bad"; such children are "good." It is clear that she is "an imp of evil" often, a stubborn little girl who refuses to recite her catechism on demand. Nonetheless, because she is beautiful and imaginative, her very being transvalues traditional notions, especially those concerning obedience and humility.

Contrast may have illuminated this vision for Hawthorne's time. In McGuffey's *Second Reader*, already widely popular, there was a lengthy story about a poor boy who plodded through life without envy of the rich, reading his Bible, helping his parents, and soberly planning to "learn accounts" so that he will be prepared if, like his father, "I shall be employed in a store." He works industriously, avoids naughty boys, is grateful for everything he receives. "When he sees little boys and girls riding on pretty horses, or in coaches, or walking with ladies and gentlemen and having on very fine clothes, he does not envy them, nor wish to be like them." He knows well that God makes some rich and some poor, and that the poor can be happy if they are good. ". . . Indeed," he says with a note of desperation, "I think that when I am good, nobody can be happier than I am."

To be good was to accept, to conform, to condemn on community grounds. To be happy was to be in accord with the majority, even if the majority needed to play at whipping Quakers, taking vengeance on an adulteress, smiling grimly if at all. (When Hawthorne described the public holiday on the occasion of the Governor's election, he noted that the people of Boston, although "not born to an inheritance of Puritan gloom," were unable to produce "more than a dim reflection of a remembered splendor, a colorless and manifold diluted repetition of what they had beheld in proud old London. . . ." Their descendants, he said, were to be even darker in mood; and, finally, making a sudden comment on his own day: "We have yet to learn again the forgotten art of gayety.")

Yet Pearl, rendered in Hawthorne's joyless time, was gay; and the image of her sets off the time's conventions in a strangely revealing light. In Hawthorne's next novel, *The House of the Seven Gables*, the antic radiance is caught in the daguerrotypes of Holgrave, who is a nineteenth-century socialist and at once a self-reliant man, living by "a law of his own." He is a critic of the "blackness" of the past, as it survives in the present, particularly in the economic arrangements of the increasingly property-conscious nineteenth century. The evils of the past are now associated with love of money—"ill-gotten gold, or real estate." The Maule curse lying over the house where the desiccated Pyncheons live is the retribution of those who have been exploited and deprived. The sterile cruelties that afflicted Hester Prynne are now identified with greed as well as bigotry.

Once Judge Pyncheon is identified as the criminal, once he dies in the windowless darkness, escape is possible for the surviving Pyncheons. The train becomes a vehicle of progress; sunshine warms the house at last. But it is left to decay and become a curiosity, because what it represents can never finally be destroyed. Like civilization itself, the past is inescapable and Janus-faced: the nature of man prevents the building of a wholly pure new world.

After making the same point in *The Blithedale Romance*, written the next year, Hawthorne wrote the campaign biography for Franklin Pierce and received a consulship in Liverpool as his reward. After spending some months in England and traveling in Italy, where he wrote *The Marble Faun*, he came home to New England again just as the Civil War began. In the preface to the novel he had written:

> No author, without a trial, can conceive the difficulty of writing a romance about a country where there is no shadow, no antiquity, no mystery, no picturesque and gloomy wrong, nor anything but a commonplace prosperity, in broad and simple daylight as is happily the case with my dear native land.

Only in the Old World, the book suggested, only among the ruins, could one perceive the "pit of blackness" so effectively screened by factuality at home.

Nevertheless, Hawthorne's art had consistently mirrored what simple daylight had screened. He had responded, since he began

to write, to the problematic aspects of that "commonplace prosperity" which presented such uncommon challenges to men,
long before the cataclysmic war. He had seen the land as pitted
and divided, with a surface "portentously heaving"; and he knew
the precariousness of institutions founded in a conviction of perfectibility and stability of forms.

New terms were needed; new inventions were required to
cope with change. Not only was this true of human beings' inner
lives; it was true of their social arrangements—their legislatures,
churches, and their schools. "We are provincial," wrote Henry
David Thoreau, "because we do not find at home our standards,
because we do not worship truth, . . . because we are warped
and narrowed by an exclusive devotion to trade and commerce
and manufactures and agriculture and the like, which are but
means, and not the end."

6

THE CLASSROOM AT
WALDEN POND

In 1854, Henry David Thoreau went to Walden Pond in the woods near Concord "to live deliberately." It was the year of Horace Mann's ninth Report, with its stress on self-government and its warning against the identification of liberty "with an absence of restraint." It was also the year of Emerson's lectures on "Representative Men," those who enabled ordinary people to feel the touch of the divine from "a higher sphere of thought."

Thoreau wanted to walk, to work, to take his time, to step "downwards through the mud and slush of opinion, and prejudice, and tradition" until he reached "hard bottom"—that which was actual and real. He liked talk; he liked visitors; but he wanted to separate himself from the life of the "herd." He would leave post offices behind him, newspapers, all the "dirty institutions" of society, including some of its schools.

But he was concerned primarily with education when he settled himself in the woods and when he returned. The chapters of *Walden*, the aphorisms in his *Journal*, the commentaries in *A Week on the Concord and Merrimack Rivers* all communicate an intense interest in finding out how human beings might learn to live. Never asking that he be taken as an example, Thoreau was trying to arouse people, to awaken them. Talking of learning what life "had to teach," he was urging them on to "conscious endeavor." If they heard, if they read, they would then try to make their own lives worthy, "to throw off sleep" at last, to heed themselves.

Thoreau was a Harvard graduate, schooled in the classics,

with some little experience teaching the young. In 1837, he had taught for two weeks in the Concord town school; but, as he told Orestes Brownson, he could not keep on because he saw no use in whipping children into righteousness. ("We should seek to be fellow-students with the pupil. . . .") Later, he and his brother established their own school in Concord; but, as they had half expected, it failed. Thoreau was not an innocent like Bronson Alcott. Even when a boy, he had understood that the community required high-sounding talk and abstract reassurance, affirmations about "the good of my fellow-men" and the rest. He had refused to oblige, even when people asked him why he taught school. He came down to the "essential fact" when he replied: to keep himself alive, he said.

He thought that everyone was "tasked to make his life . . . worthy of the contemplation of his most-elevated and critical hour," and this meant that human beings could not be *taught* to live worthily, to be good. The existing society seemed to him to be full of dullness, detail, and pointless labor. He said that it burdened men too heavily to allow them the time for free and happy lives. But this did not mean that he hoped to change it, or that he founded his hopes on some new, improved communal design. Individuals had to liberate themselves, not depend on society to do it for them.

To think of saving people by building utopias seemed to him meaningless—just as meaningless as deliberately nurturing morality. Mann, for example, talked of acclimating men morally to American institutions and, by doing so, equipping them to be free. Thoreau did not see much difference among those who spoke of *making* people virtuous. Whether the moralist was a Mann, a McGuffey, or a Robert Owen, he was overlooking the essentials. Goodness, to Thoreau, was but the natural expression of being alive in an "infinite expectation of the dawn. . . ." The person who lived wholesomely, cheerfully, simply, would grow spontaneously, and no one need concern himself about such a person's morality.

Thoreau wrote of cold, pure water, the smooth white stones

around a pond, the feel of bricks, the taste of bread, the smell of
pipe smoke, fires, early morning—the perfume of a yellow birch.
He devoted an entire chapter to "Sounds": the locomotive whis-
tle like the scream of a hawk; the bell in the silences; the secret
beat of hills and fields. *Walden* is permeated with evocations of
music in variable rhythms: the pounding of progress, the clang-
ing of machines, and the sound of a man's own drumbeat, heard
in the inner ear. ("If a man does not keep pace with his companions, perhaps it is because he hears a different drummer. Let
him step to the music which he hears, however measured or far
away.")

The din of social living, wherever carried on, seemed to
Thoreau to drown out the beat of authenticity. This was another
reason for his leaving, for two years, the village with its talk and
gossip and din. He was not an antisocial man, however, not a self-
complete single self. When he was in New York in 1843, he had
complained often of loneliness among "the herds of men," of his
inability to meet any "real and living person." Whenever he
found such a person, he remained involved with him; and, living
in the woods, he kept close touch with his good friends. He returned to Concord regularly for meals, visits, refuge from the
cold. He took his long walks with companions rather than alone.
He never pretended to be a Robinson Crusoe, dependent wholly
on himself.

His object was to take time to listen to himself, to find words
that would truly render his subject matter. He had chosen himself for subject matter because that was what he knew best, but
in expressing it he was imaging a representative man as well. To
be representative, as Thoreau saw it, was not to be greater or
larger than others. It signified a distillation of what was elemen-
tal in the ordinary, the "common" man. Sometimes he meant the
"new man," the American, who might well be happier "sauntering" through the world than exerting power over it in his pursuit
of material things.

He was, Thoreau suggested, enacting every individual's rebel-
lion, in order to stir others into action, protest, choice. He would

arouse people from their "lives of quiet desperation" and the re-signed conviction that "there is no choice left." He would move them to give up reliance on authority and opinion, to encounter life as "an experiment to a great extent untried."

With such intentions, he pointed to the meaninglessness of busy-work, artificial social contacts, material ambitions, eti-quette, brittle forms. He told over and over what it would be like to be free of all that, active, attuned to the rhythms of the succu-lent earth. Those who heeded needed only to be willing to "live sincerely" and "with the license of a higher order of beings" to take long strides and stand tall.

Unlike Hawthorne, he did not see mankind forever limited by a "haunted mind." Once men were free to be themselves, he thought, they would become as moral and brotherly as human beings had ever been. When he left the woods for any reason, he said, or when he spent his night in the city jail, he did not worry about his possessions or his property. He knew people would come by while he was away, but he was convinced they would all respect what he had: "I am convinced, that if all men were to live as simply as I then did, thieving and robbery would be unknown. These take place in communities where some have got more than is sufficient, while others have not enough." All that was needed, he pointed out, was that the leaders of the people be vir-tuous. The common men could be relied upon to be virtuous in their turn.

This was closer to the Jeffersonian notion of "moral sense" than it was to Hawthorne's conception or to Horace Mann's. Thoreau was in many ways more optimistic than Hawthorne, since he was willing to do away with laws and codes and trust to the law of man's own being. He was not concerned with breaking the "magnetic chain" so long as men were free to feel their or-ganic kinship and were not exploited by their fellow men. Hawthorne, too, was finding greed and ownership a curse; but he did not believe, as Thoreau seemed to, that they could be wholly eradicated if Americans set themselves free.

Thoreau differed with Mann as the Transcendentalists differed with him; the "compliance" the schoolmen spoke of seemed to him a mockery of true morality. Yet, in another sense, he would have had to agree that people had to be conditioned to the "self-control" society demanded—indoctrinated in the official virtues, which to him meant cowering, sneaking, living in "tedium and ennui." It seemed unnatural for youngsters to be asked to enter a society in which so many people were "well-nigh crushed and smothered under their load" of property and responsibility—and where others became their own slavedrivers, victims of their success. "It is hard," he wrote, "to have a Southern overseer; it is worse to have a Northern one; but worst of all when you are the slave-driver of yourself."

Where labor was concerned, Thoreau saw no real difference between chattel slavery and wage labor. His interest was directed to men's self-images, to which he called the "private opinion" which could dehumanize as effectively as chains or the opinion of the crowd. He did not believe that most people were strong enough to cope with the pressures of society while abiding by its codes. "In the long run men hit only what they aim at. Therefore, though they should fail immediately, they had better aim at something high." The factory owners were degraded by aiming at profit rather than at what they needed simply to live well. The factory workers were degraded by being used and exploited so that "the corporations may be enriched"—and by acceding to an inferior estimate of themselves. Poor and driven though they were, they too often forgot that they required no more than the necessities of life. Foolishly, often unnecessarily, wrote Thoreau, they resigned themselves to lifetimes of drudgery, duty, and discontent.

He chose the example nearest at hand to make his point about the workingman's plight. There were railroad tracks near Walden Pond, and he had watched the Irish laborers working day after day. Again, having heard, having seen, he defined himself as he found words. The tracks, he wrote, and the railroad cars had been built at the cost of human lives; Irish workers were sleeping below. He described those who worked along the tracks to keep the roadbed smooth; "it takes a gang of men for every five miles to keep the sleepers down and level in their beds as it is, for this is a sign that they may sometime get up again." He asked whether men really believed it was worthwhile to build railroads, just so that some could ride cheaply and fast:

> . . . but though a crowd rushes to the depot, and the conductor shouts "All aboard!" when the smoke is blown away and the vapor condensed, it will be perceived that a few are riding, but the rest are run over—and it will be called, and will be, "A melancholy accident." No doubt they can ride at last who shall have earned their fare, that is, if they survive so long, but they will probably have lost their elasticity and desire to travel by that time. This spending of the best part of one's life earning money in order to enjoy a questionable liberty during the least part of it reminds me of the Englishman who went to India to make a fortune first, in order that he might return . . . and live the life of a poet. He should have gone up garret at once.

Then he pictured the "million Irishmen starting up from all the shanties in the land" to ask whether railroad-building were not a good thing to do. He would answer *"comparatively good"*; but, as human beings, they might have spent their lives better "than digging in this dirt."

Thoreau was not asserting that "so-called internal improvements" were *ipso facto* bad. He was not asking that everyone choose the simple life and retire to the woods. He was challenging his contemporaries to examine their lives and their commitments, to consider the values they were pursuing. To ask whether it is worthwhile to spend time decorating houses, manufacturing ornaments, struggling to accumulate the superfluous, is not to say such activities are wrong. As we have seen, Thoreau did not think anyone could be taught a viable morality, even the morality of spontaneous growth. He was not persuading his readers to accept his estimate of what was right and wrong; he was trying to make them consider their major premises, to ask questions even about the progress and improvement of which they were so proud. When he associated these with the "hurry and waste of life" he saw about him, he was attempting to engage people emotionally, sensually, in confrontation. This was why he chose the images of automatons and burdened, trudging creatures, why he contrasted these with images of hikers and "surveyors" of woods and ponds. To be an Indian scout, a trailbreaker, a sauntering woodsman, was to belong to indigenous tradition. Thoreau knew, as American writers since have seemed to know, that images like those were linked to men's feelings about freedom, about manhood. Evoking them as he did, he was insisting upon what he took to be the individual heart's desire. Opposing them to what Americans had become, he was insisting that the individual look again, consult his dream, consider what was lost.

Figurative, nondidactic as Thoreau's writing is, it may have been the writing of a teacher. We have discovered that to teach is not, by definition, to impose a code or a way of life—that it can be a process of enabling students to learn. If to learn is to integrate new knowledge with what is already known, if it is to organize one's experience and make one's own sense of the world, then Thoreau was as concerned with goading people to learn as he was with making them feel.

Because of his indifference to existing schools, it is sometimes forgotten that he was profoundly interested in schooling; his peculiarly erudite preoccupations are often set aside. There was an intrinsic value in learning, as he saw it, which made studying and inquiry essential to full human growth. Part of his objection to the contemporary society was due to its provincialism. He saw knowledge being misused and pigeonholed when it was justified merely as "power," as an instrumentality for gaining success. The habit of learning to read "to serve a paltry convenience" appalled him. He objected bitterly to learning to cipher "in order to keep accounts and not be cheated in trade."

He wanted to see people read the classics for their own sake and to know the languages of Greece and Rome. He appealed to the farmers around him and the villagers of Concord to forsake the newspapers they read so constantly, the dime novels, the trivia of journalism, and to plunge into the great literature of the ages. He saw this not as a mode of self-improvement or as a way of learning Truth. To read was another way of opening oneself to the world and the possibilities in the world. It could lead to an awakening, to taking a new, a creative chance.

To read this way, to engage in the past and make it one's own, was to see oneself in perspective, to extend life beyond routine. Thoreau would have liked to see the whole of existence as an activity of reaching out to the horizons. Education was not intended for children alone. It ought to continue, he thought, through a man's entire lifetime; it ought to be, as John Dewey would one day say, "life itself." If this were to happen, the very texture of village civilization would change. There would be a democratic renaissance of learning in towns throughout the land. They might begin playing the role once played by noblemen in Renaissance Europe; they might be transformed into "noble villages of men," where scholars were supported and endowed, where perpetual "uncommon schools" would provide ongoing education to all the citizens, no matter what their occupations, no matter how old they were. He knew "it is thought Utopian to propose spending money" for something men would think impractical. But the proposal itself might be a challenge (as all Thoreau's ideas were intended to be) to men in need of self-examination, to people caught in a barren world:

> We have a comparatively decent system of common schools, schools for infants only; but excepting the half-starved Lyceum in the winter, and latterly the puny beginning of a library suggested by the state, no school for ourselves. We spend more on almost any article of bodily aliment or ailment than on our mental aliment. It is time that we had uncommon schools, that we did not leave off our education when we begin to be men and women. It is time that villages were universities. . . .

On Civil Disobedience, too, may be taken to be a challenge, another goad to people to take responsibility for themselves. When Thoreau described the injustice of majorities, or when he spoke of the inexpediency of the majority of governments, he was not asking his fellow citizens either to protest or to separate themselves. When he refused to pay his poll tax and spent his night in jail, he was not acting for the public good or to bring about social change. "I simply wish," he said, "to refuse allegiance to the State, to withdraw and stand aloof from it effectually." The reason was that the state had permitted itself to be used by those who wanted a war with Mexico and by those who profited from slavery. To "stand aloof" was to make a private gesture—and to challenge others to confront responsibility.

Quietly, as he put it later, he declared war on the state. He signed a statement affirming that he "did not wish to be regarded as a member of any incorporated society" which he had not freely joined. He was willing to give up protection by the state, since acceptance of it seemed to make him nothing but an instrument or tool. He would live, he wrote, by his private conscience and act, when he had to, upon its claims. This was simply another expression of his determination to march to his own music, to obey his own law. Placing himself above the Constitution and the enacted laws, he was once again asking people to think—to consider who and what they were.

It happened that he was writing about civil disobedience at the time Horace Mann was preparing to leave his Secretaryship and go to Washington. Like many other men, Mann and Thoreau were both prone to see slavery as the key to the time's immorality; and, distinctive as they were, they both consulted attitudes toward slavery when evaluating the way things were. Thoreau asked the question crucial for the schools, however, where slavery was concerned: "This American government—what is it but a tradition, though a recent one, endeavoring to transmit itself unimpaired to posterity, but each instant losing some of its integrity?" Integrity, as Thoreau saw it, was a function of the government's handling of slave-state demands; but his question related to an even larger one: what was a morally oriented school to do in an increasingly immoral world?

There were intimations in Thoreau's own writing, hints at alternative modes of educating—teaching children not to comply but to think and be themselves. The uncertainties, however, would persist for generations. Americans would be torn between the desire for gain and the desire to follow impulse and go sauntering in the woods, just as they would be torn between the brute excitements of corporate growth and the defense of laissez faire.

Whatever resolutions could be found would be, in time, incorporated in the schools, since it was largely in the schools that Americans were to learn how and what to be. There would be empiricists like Thoreau who would devote attention to deliberate living within the schools; there would be others who would conceive the heritage as subject matter and work to give it point and form. But for years there would be uncertainty about the America that was or ought to be in the making. Was it to be a nation of freeholders, working, walking to their own drumbeats? Was it to be a nation of efficient organizations, demanding competence above all things, discipline—compliance with regulations governing the whole?

"However intense my experience," Thoreau once wrote, "I am conscious of the presence and criticism of a part of me, which, as it were, is not a part of me, but spectator, sharing no experience, but taking note of it, and that is no more I than it is you. When the play—and it may be the tragedy of life—is over, the spectator goes his way." Perhaps the free individual was to be the spectator; perhaps the best the school could do was enable him to understand, to "take note," to impose his own particular form while the machines and progress clanked on. No one could be sure; but the school would have to take the risk of trying—always and always looking both ways.

7

MASSES, MELTING-POTS,
AND MONITORS
"Rote" Teaching and Lancastrian Schools

Beyond the woods there were the uncertainties of expansion and the impersonal thud of change. In the 1840s and 1850s, thousands of miles of railroad track were flung across the country. Abruptly the North and the West became interdependent; the demands of a national economy began dominating the lives of men. Crude economic power was held by the railroad industry; within the first decade of its growth, that power began to be wielded against hundreds of Midwest communities, against settlers who had thought of themselves as autonomous, against a government too credulous to resist.

The railroads also made material demands, and numerous subsidiary industries grew up in response. With opportunity so vast and profits so unprecedented, fraud and corruption became commonplace. Efficiency and expediency became the criteria as novel industries developed and spread. There seemed no other way to keep up, to progress. Christian morals, even Transcendentalist morals, seemed irrelevant in a world where machines were being invented daily, assembly lines being extended, more and more laborers being sucked into the mills.

Everything seemed to be in flux; men needed a sense that something endured. Many were like adolescents, breaking the bonds of the familiar and at once hanging on. Not only was the transition explosive; it seemed to some to have escaped human expectation and control. And it was inescapable, even for those who remained where they had always been, on the land. At one moment they were living in a handicraft economy, in wooden houses with woodburning stoves. At the next moment, coal, copper, iron appeared. Cotton mills began using steam; shipwrights began sheathing ships with copper; an engineering industry was launched; agricultural machinery was manufactured in the West. News came from international fairs of cables and vulcanization, fast-moving threshing machines, a telegraph, newer and newer tools.

The population was increasing: between 1840 and 1860, it jumped by 14,500,000 to 31,500,000. As the railroads promoted regional specialization, cities began growing more rapidly than before. By the Civil War, almost one quarter of the American people lived in urban centers of at least 2500 inhabitants. And the immigrants poured in, as many as 430,000 in 1854 alone. Many went out to Midwest farms, but the cities and the factories continued to attract tens of thousands. The markets for produce increased, but so did the ills of the cities. The annexation of new territories, the issue of slavery, the Fugitive Slave Act began creating fissures throughout the North and the West, By 1854 the people were becoming realigned, and a Republican party was formed by antislavery Democrats (like Thoreau and Hawthorne) and Whigs like Horace Mann. Know-Nothingism became a national movement: the Order of the Star-Spangled Banner, organized in New York, was transformed into the American Party, which grew for two years until it too broke up on the issue of slavery.

No place so resembled a barometer of the time as did New York. There, every rise and fall in production was registered, every shift in the pressure of trade, every tidal movement in the struggle over slavery, every pulsation in the nation's effort to impose its will on the world.

By the second decade of the century, the city of New York was the most powerful in the country; the state was as populous as all the New England states. The opening of the Erie Canal insured that the port of New York would continue the most prosperous in the East. Wealth and power mushroomed in both city and state. Immigrants converged on Manhattan: Germans, then thousands of Irish, raveling the antique brocade of Dutch and English life.

Utopian and radical activities proliferated until midcentury. There was a religious community at Oneida, where the disciples spoke of electing Jesus Christ President of the World. An anti-Masonic party exerted influence in upstate hamlets and villages. There were the angry Know-Nothings, resisting the incursions of "foreigners." There was a radicalism that sometimes overlapped the more orthodox political movements; and growing numbers of people were engaging themselves in fighting for causes as national and religious groups identified each other and began to contend.

Every shift and swing on the national scene seemed to be magnified once it was felt in New York. Antimonopoly Locofocos organized to fight the Whigs. They were joined by Barnburners, Democrats of all persuasions, until in the 1840s radical Democracy regained control in the state. Ex-President Van Buren, head of the Democratic majority, formed a Free Soil and Anti-Slavery Party (like the one whose candidate Horace Mann became), but here it was devoted to Jacksonian ideals, to the idea of the "majority," to assuring the people their own voice.

Customary dividing lines could never be firmly drawn. The immigrants, continually irritating native Protestants, had to be somehow assuaged as their numbers swelled. The corporations, still described as "monsters" by the Jacksonians, had to be handled delicately, because they were bulwarks of prosperity and promoters of the railroads and the canals. Antislavery, the most magnetic and divisive cause of all, had to be qualified by the need to make money, because Southern cotton was shipped by the ton through New York harbor and its returns were keeping thousands in their jobs.

Discord and ambiguity were reflected even in the physical appearance of New York City. The rutted, unpaved streets boasted the finest mansions in the North and the most dilapidated slums. Bands of vicious dogs ran through the alleys and among the carriage wheels on the avenues. There were hogpens on empty lots, and scavenger pigs were continually breaking out to forage in back gardens or on the thoroughfares. Immigrants were pressed against one another in barracks or in dwellings underground, with saloons in the cellars, betting parlors, vice, all the trappings of despair. When Charles Dickens visited the city, he found the Five Points district unique in the world for prostitution, alcoholism, and disease.

Vast warehouses lined the waterfront, encasing the extravagances of the streets. In spite of them, in spite of offices, banks, and the rituals of a prosperous mercantile world, the atmosphere was often that of a brawling frontier settlement. The West opened up across the Hudson River; forests impinged on the northern farms; to the east and south there was the sea. But New York could not withdraw behind stockades of orthodoxy; nor could it bind itself safely in universally agreed-upon codes. A multiverse since its beginnings, it was by now a web of separate communities, lacking social and moral coherence, without a sense of common goals.

In the upstate rural areas, conditions differed, and the difference was exemplified most sharply in the arrangements made for schools. Under the Dutch and in the early years of English control, the villages of New York had been established by a great variety of national groups, each tending to create a replica of its old-country way of life. Many were Dutch Reformed, recapitulating the history of Geneva—or of Massachusetts Bay. Some were German Pietist, some Norwegian Lutheran or French Huguenot; others were English, both Dissenter and High Church. The important thing was that each was internally homogeneous, almost always parochial, moved by a provincial desire to be itself as history advanced. This did not, in most cases, necessarily find expression in a willingness to support town schools; but, when the French immigrants became numerous and New Englanders began filtering in after the Revolutionary War, demands for some sort of comprehensive school system began increasingly to be raised.

In 1805 a state school fund was established; in 1812 a comprehensive school law was passed. Each district was required to tax itself an amount to match state moneys derived from interest on the fund. When there were deficits, the districts were permitted, as in New England, to charge rates, except where individual parents were too poor to pay. Although this put off the day when the schools would be free and the stigma of pauperism removed, foundations were being laid for locally controlled common schools throughout the state, despite the fact that state interest waxed and waned. The exception, however, was the City of New York.

There the philanthropic tradition survived long. In 1805 a group of charitable citizens had formed an association for the raising of subscriptions to pay for free schools for the poor, and the Free School Society then formed bore the responsibility for popular education for more than twenty years. When the school fund was established, the city's share was paid to the Society, three smaller associations, and any religious societies applying for aid to charity schools. In 1826, the Society was renamed the Public School Society and given the right to levy taxes in the city, thus taking over the functions of a secular agency appointed to take charge of common schools.

As the population increased, however, numerous religious groups began beleaguering the legislature with demands for fiscal powers like those of the Society. The Catholic Church, confronting a tidal wave of Catholic immigration, exerted strong pressure; and, in 1840, Governor William H. Seward (later Lincoln's Secretary of State) delivered an inaugural address which included a proposal for aid to Catholic elementary schools in a blanket proposal for expanded common schools throughout the state. As Seward saw it, the common school idea implied that every child was to be educated "in all the elements of knowledge we possess." He reasoned that parochial education too would in time promote the emergence of a "homogeneous people," so long as Church schools worked with the common schools toward a shared community end. Troubled by the spectacle of Catholic children without schools to go to, he overlooked existing preoc-

cupations with the moral function of education. And he under-
estimated the strength of the disagreements over what that
moral function should be.

The controversy was fed by some of the enthusiasms left from
the Workingmen's Party's agitation for schools in the 1830s.
Frances Wright and Robert Owen's son, Robert Dale Owen, had
linked demands for equal opportunity with demands for humane, Pestalozzian public schools; and, although support declined after the 1837 depression began, there were memories of
the eloquent talk about equality and about a "republican" system
of education sanctioned by a secular creed.

The Church's prime objection to the free schools in New York,
however, was that they were dominated by the "Protestant principle," for all the Public School Society's nonsectarian claims.
The Society's charter, for one thing, still spoke of "centralized
Protestant control"; for another, and more seriously, the Protestant Bible was regularly read in the Society's schools. Catholic
children would not have been permitted to attend schools without religious teaching; but the Church stressed the sectarianism
of the existing schools in order to bolster its demands for public
aid to its own institutions—and to their teaching of the "Authority," a dogma in many ways at odds with the majority faith.

Governor Seward's proposal was rejected, and in 1841 both
the New York City Council and the legislature turned aside the
demands of all religious groups for aid to sectarian schools. In
1842 the legislature caused a Board of Education to be established in the city, to set up and operate a system of locally controlled, nonsectarian free schools. Although the Society did not
dissolve until 1853, its schools were placed under the Board's jurisdiction; in a short time religious teaching was effectively outlawed in tax-supported schools. Private and parochial institutions
were allowed to exist, but the promise of state financial aid was
removed.

Tension and uncertainty, however, could not be outlawed. On
occasion, during the forties, there were Catholic riots in the

streets. Important, though not always visible, was the sense of unease with respect to moral training, now to be carried on in an undefined and unfamiliar secular language. In a city so multifarious and exposed, the problem was more acute than in Massachusetts, where Horace Mann could appeal to the "good sense of the community" when he was attacked by the fathers of the churches. Unlike his opposite numbers in New York, he could assume consensus in his constituency, such that "all good schools and good teachers would be safe" from orthodox attack.

Loyalties remained too provincial in New York for such consensus to be assumed. It was true that the state had contributed much to the cause of common schools: the country's earliest board of education, the second American normal school. The long existence of state laws showed that men had been fighting for a generation for tax-supported education; at midcentury, many were still battling the rate bill heroically, struggling to overcome the pauper approach. Radical Democrats had begun speaking of common schools again as "a republican necessity." Certain businessmen were beginning to speak of them as the guardians of public order and volunteering tax support without their traditional complaints.

Without the Puritan background that supported the moralism in the Massachusetts schools, the city schoolmen depended for many years on the Lancastrian system of education, which was expected to have the same effect. Joseph Lancaster had come to the United States soon after the turn of the century with news of a set of techniques he had developed in England (and Andrew Bell had developed in India) for use in institutions for children of the poor. It struck many people as an efficient, businesslike system of mass education, and for several years those who hoped to see philanthropy continue to educate the poor expected that Lancastrianism would stave off taxation for free schools.

Nothing could be cheaper or neater than a system which made it possible for one teacher to instruct five hundred or more children at one time. This was the secret of its attraction. It involved the "monitorial" device—dependence upon squads of children deputized as monitors, each assigned a specific task in the activity of instruction, drill, or discipline.

The teacher typically faced a vast and echoing assembly hall, far larger and more barren than the Massachusetts one-room schools. Sometimes it was crammed with nearly a thousand children, ranked in rows of twenty or more. The jobs of hearing lessons or administering tests were done by the monitors, who reported through their squad leaders to the teacher at the head of the line. Other monitors policed the room, carried out punishments, reported wrongdoings, carried messages and instructions from the teacher to the deputies assigned to each charted and numbered row.

The textbooks and the curricula were similar to those in Massachusetts, as was the general methodology. But here the assembly-line principle governed. Discipline was coldly enforced, sometimes with the aid of cruel punishment. When the Bible was read, the words echoed hollowly in the barnlike rooms. Nevertheless, this was the official method adopted by the Public School Society, and it was in use until after the Civil War in New York and in other large cities, except in New England, where the approach was considered too crude.

To many people, this was the only viable method of imposing order and "good habits" on disreputable immigrant children from so many of the countries in the Western world. It was a mode of riot control, an economical business practice; and, in New York, expediency had long been used to resolve conflicts in the absence of consentient principle. Few prophetic moralists climbed the hustings on behalf of the children in the automatized schools. Few urban reformers worked to relate what was happening there to expressed community commitments. Liberals like Horace Greeley were skeptical of the schools in any case because of the class differences among the children, the economic inequalities they thought no common school could ever allay. Transcendentally inclined idealists like Albert Brisbane and Henry James Senior had too little confidence in the Establishment to expect any good from public schools being sponsored by a materialist "civilization." If "community" were to be attained, they thought, New Yorkers and Americans had to find another way.

By midcentury, it happened that two men, both born in 1819 in New York, were prepared to point a way. They were Herman Melville and Walt Whitman, both of whom were already shaping images of the American condition more vigorously and daringly than any artists had done before. But they were deeply different from one another, in that Melville had chosen to engage himself with "blackness," and Whitman to catalogue identities and "miracles"—to affirm. If their voices were to be heard in chorus, the contrapuntal sound of a nation at adolescence would be audible very soon. The dissonance of alienation would make the music rougher than any Thoreau had heard or played; but harmonies of new identification—perhaps on another scale— would be heard under the counterpoint. And, whether or not they were composed with children's voices in mind, they would carry a potential in them for the meanings and the sounds in common schools.

8

"... HIGH TIME TO GO TO SEA. ..."
Melville's Vision of America

"The transition is a keen one, I assure you, from a schoolmaster to a sailor. ..." This was Herman Melville speaking through Ishmael in *Moby-Dick*. Just as certain schoolmasters can discover their true identities on board ship, so can aspects of the American school be made clear if viewed through the perspective of an artist-seaman, especially one making "blubber into poetry."

Melville was born in the whirl of New York. He was heir to a structured Dutch tradition through his mother and her prosperous family. His childhood was spent among his relatives, the Gansevoorts, and he was given an almost tribal sense of belonging to a people who had been successful since the beginning of New World history. When he was eleven, however, his father suffered a business failure; and the Melvilles moved to Albany where, two years later, the father died. Herman spent two dislocated years working in a shop; then, at seventeen, he went off on a disheartening journey to Liverpool, where he seemed to see only people who were poor. When he returned, he taught briefly in a district school; when he came of age in 1841 he returned to the sea, this time on a whaling ship bound for the Pacific islands.

The trip was to provide the themes for his novels *Typee* and *Omoo* and to be the first of the voyages which would make him see in whaling ships "my Yale College and my Harvard." His ship's master was brutal. Life was harsh among the depraved sailors on the *Acushnet*; after a year and a half, Melville and a shipmate jumped ship in the Marquesas Islands, where they spent four weeks among the "savages." After they escaped, they were taken aboard an Australian whaler; they went through a mutiny, to jail in Tahiti, and landed at last in Hawaii. After working in Honolulu for a time, Melville found a berth on a frigate and returned to New York in 1844.

More important than the experiences he had had was the enlargement they underwent in Melville's imagination, an enlargement that enabled him not only to render native island life for its own sake, but to form it in contrast to the lives of the Liverpool slum-dwellers and of the brutish sailors with whom he had sailed. This meant that, because of chance and circumstance, he was able to begin his writing career in a dimension of experience like the one Hawthorne had explored: the borderland between maypole and whipping post, savage innocence and the rules of civilization.

In *Typee*, the islanders he remembered became the "pure and upright" Typees, leading an indolent, innocent life in a tropical Happy Valley, immune to the hypocrisies of civilized men. They strike the hero of the tale as exotic, spontaneous creatures, like the "noble savage" of the eighteenth century. He is cared for by them, and he falls in love with one of their girls. Then, abruptly, he stumbles upon a "Taboo grove" and realizes that his kindly host and beautiful lady may well be cannibals. "Ambiguities" begin to trouble him; at length he runs away from the Happy Valley to the more sophisticated, less humane world of the mercenary and the civilized, where he belongs.

Omoo was intended as a satire of the French colonialists and missionaries in Tahiti. They are shown wooing the islanders clownishly, immorally, with the goods and devices of Christianity and the West. The simple natives are depraved by the imposition of alien standards. They are forced into postures of deceit, deprived of the pride and wholeness they possessed when they were free to follow instinct and live in simple innocence.

Like Hawthorne, Melville was pointing to the arbitrariness of orthodoxies; but he went further and explored the questionable character of any claim to universality. There was a consciousness of paradox in his treatment of the missionaries' pride and the natives' problematic simplicity. Inculcation of a foreign way of life seemed always to be wrong, but it was impossible to take a stand against indoctrination with a knowledge of what the Typees had secreted in the grove.

It is just possible that Melville's sense of dichotomy was in some respect a function of his memories of New York. He had looked out upon the streets and slums of the metropolis from a middle-class eyrie, where he was protected against the tensions of melting-pot life. He had been tutored by a governess and been sent to the New York Male High School, which catered only to the well-to-do. But he had lived in the midst of the city and been conscious of it churning around him. He had gone back to it on several occasions when he was grown—to look for work before shipping off to the South Seas, to see literary friends while trying to learn how to write.

Enough experience lay behind him to account for his concern with slum degradations and the strains of cultural difference, which became a kind of *leitmotif* in his work. He never explicitly decried the city in itself; nor did he imagine people becoming "naturally" virtuous if they were set free to roam the woods. He began *Moby-Dick*, however, with the "insular city of the Man-hattoes," the city where crowds of landsmen, "tied to counters, nailed to benches, clinched to desks" on weekdays, come to stare at the sea on Sunday afternoons. And his story "Bartleby the Scrivener" was to deal with a young stranger lost in a lawyer's office on Wall Street, and with a respectable city man feeling "the bond of a common humanity" and drawn "irresistibly to gloom."

Islands, cities, outsiders; men tied and nailed and clinched— surely some of this was a response to a fragmented world. It was, particularly in the cities, a world of strangers, of diverse cultures. The public schools, assigned the responsibility of creating a "common" heritage, inducting into a "common" culture, could not avoid making the suspect claims of the missionaries in Tahiti. They too were imposing an alien way of life on distinctive groups of children, a "respectable" way, godly and in many senses inhumane.

Thoreau, at Walden Pond, said "Simplify!" Melville's universe was already too complex for simple contraries or dualities. His third book, written after his marriage in 1847, dealt with a "chartless" voyage in search of the meaning of life. This was the involuted, poetic *Mardi*; it was a sign that some deep-sea explorations were about to begin, an annunciation of the mood that would lead to *Moby-Dick*.

Two realistic sea stories intervened: "Redburn," with its description of a boy's initiation into evil and cruelty, and "White Jacket," with its exposure of brutalities on Navy ships, its view of mankind as the crew of a "world-frigate" sailing under sealed orders, with secrets in her storerooms and her hold. An aesthetic initiation also intervened. Melville read the work of William Shakespeare, "full of sermons-on-the-mount," he said, "and gentle, aye, almost as Jesus." The plays led him to other Elizabethan dramas, to seventeenth- and eighteenth-century literature. He read the Bible over and over; in climax, he read Greek tragedies.

Like Thoreau, he had discovered the possibility of intense personal experience by means of the classics. For Melville, however, it was not simply a matter of voyaging outward: like a true sailor, he had eventually to return. Traveling was purposeful; he was accustomed to going in search of fish, produce, whale oil—and to coming back with riches of some sort, riches that could be put to work. So he put to work what he had caught in the years of reading and pondering as well as in the years of sailing, of becoming an artist and a man. Like a nineteenth-century Ulysses, he treated what he had found as a series of revelations, valuable not only for their own sake, but because they helped him discover the coastlines and islands of the inexplicable, enticing world—and because they enabled him to come home again and endeavor to remake, to renew.

Most of this took place below the level of consciousness—or so it appears when we see it all surge upward after Melville's reading of Hawthorne's short stories and his mountain meetings with Hawthorne and his family. The communion with Hawthorne (who knew, Melville had written, "the great power of blackness") is taken to be the explanation of Melville's decision to rewrite a half-completed novel about two men on a realistic whaling voyage, to create the mysterious bulk we know as *Moby-Dick*.

To venture into *Moby-Dick* for any purpose is to venture into a many-layered universe, a domain of half-lights, of mysteries. To do this with the public schools in mind is to chart a path somewhat arbitrarily, to categorize warily—and to leave the way open for a variety of interpretations of the work and its ultimate incomprehensibility. Just as all Melville's previous works hold the potentialities for this one, so in some sense do the works of Hawthorne and Thoreau—and so does the New England *Primer* with its "Whales in the Sea," its talk of "Deluge" and of "Pride." The novel is a great white landmark in our history; and, in the distances, like the outline of a continent, the tragedies and epics of the West loom up behind. For the first time "this new man, this American" was about to enter what Melville called "the common continent of men."

There are no answers in *Moby-Dick*, however, no solutions or correctives. There are only vantage points: mastheads, quarter deck, forecastle, whaleboat, coffin, and a vortex subsiding "to a creamy pool." Because such vantage points are not the customary ones for those concerned with the problem of schools, new angles and planes are likely to appear when they are taken; new meanings are likely to emerge. Much depends on the questions defined, and *Moby-Dick* can instigate a hundred questions, many of them having to do with value and truth and the nature of man, all matters relevant to schools.

There is the matter of the individual in America and of the nature of the community that may someday be achieved. There is the issue of the knowledge to be transmitted—the knowledge that is power, enlightenment, or doom. There is the question of morality and what it is to be humane. And there are the complex problems of relationship, not only among men but also among distinctive ways of life. And the pervasive problem of keeping a world alive and afloat, with multiple fulfillments being sought, and shifting truths, and (as educators too must understand) the need for confrontation of "the whiteness of the whale."

The book begins with the demand for identification: "Call me Ishmael." It is not difficult today to identify with the Biblical wanderer, the outsider. It may not be too difficult either to identify with someone "growing grim about the mouth," someone who senses "a damp, drizzly November in his soul." But these are not identifications familiar to the practicing schoolman, with his views of commonalty and his high, melioristic hopes. They may move him immediately to consider his premises, to experience his doubts, to articulate his conception of equality. They may even move him to define somewhat more clearly his image of man, of the "democratic character" he is to create in his school. And if he is moved to do none of these things, he may still respond to Ishmael's "pausing before coffin warehouses" and going to sea as a "substitute for pistol and ball." Ishmael is a city man and melancholy; he does not know who he is.

It becomes clear very soon that this is to be a tale about the making of a self, about refashioning the form of a life. Ishmael, like Thoreau, is embarking on an effort to learn, to be educated; but his classroom will be a "wonder-world," the open wastes of the sea.

He takes his carpet bag and travels to New Bedford in search of a berth; first there is his mistaken plunge into the dark world of wailing, the Negro church behind the sign labeled THE TRAP. When he reaches the Spouter-Inn, he is given a bed with Queequeg, a stranger more frightening than any in *Typee*. But there is contact; there is communion, and Ishmael's isolation begins to give way: "—the man's a human being just as I am. . . ." (Is not that Everyman's beginning in any human school?) In the morning, Ishmael awakens in Queequeg's "bridegroom clasp." There is acceptance, now, of one level of selfhood, the simplest one, the instinctual level; they can stroll freely through the summer daylight of the town.

The Whaleman's Chapel and the sermon offered by Father

Mapple provide further clues, pointers to the core of the book. The sermon, dealing ostensibly with Jonah and the whale, concerns the soul, the selfhood of Everyman—and the "delight" which comes to him who "ever stands forth his own inexorable self." True delight, Father Mapple says, "top-gallant delight," comes to him "who acknowledges no law or lord, but the Lord his God, and is only a patriot to heaven." But his is not simply the traditional reminder that man must lose himself in God to find himself. Nor is it the Christian insistence upon humility before the single God.

In the following chapter, Ishmael watches Queequeg worship his idol and asks himself about the meaning of worship, and about whether a good Presbyterian can join in Queequeg's pagan rituals. When he decides that worship is but to do the will of God and that the will of God is "to do to my fellow man what I would have my fellow man do to me . . . ," he kneels down next to Quee-queg because Queequeg is his fellow man.

This act of affirmation prepares for conflicts and resolutions to come, but it is also a further response to the question of cultural difference posed in Melville's early novels. Also, it is an announcement of the idea that the full development of a man's "own inexorable self" (his identity, perhaps) is connected with his ability to be a brother-man. Just as this relates to what Hawthorne and Thoreau were saying, so does it touch the perplexities of those seeking a "common" moral ideal for the public school. There were already indications that the school would have to concern itself with something more than "social principle." Before long, such men as Francis Parker, G. Stanley Hall, and John Dewey would be attending to the individuality of the child who might grow up to be tied, nailed—crucified—by the demands of Trade. It would not be sufficient to talk of compliance and conformity then, or of conventional worship of a single God. Individuals would have to be freed for growth—as Ishmaels and Queequegs—and, in their inexorable distinctiveness, discover mutual regard.

By the time Ishmael and Queequeg board the *Pequod*, the

quest for a mode of standing forth is well under way. Each crew member turns out to be an island man, an "Isolato living on a separate continent of his own." Because of Ishmael's inner and outer alienation, he confronts his shipmates as potential resources in the shaping of his own identity, and as potential comrades who will help him become whole.

The crew members appear to be exemplars of the range of human drives and energies. They seem to inhabit all the levels of consciousness available to a living man. Taken individually, no one of them could pilot a ship, harpoon a whale, raise a sail. Yet as a crew, a "deputation" from mankind, they can sail a ship with a "grand, ungodly, godlike" Captain at the helm. They are called "knights and squires," these islanders seeking whales. They represent the problematic "new man"—and, like the American of Melville's own time, they have found it impossible to become integrated selves, to be unified and whole.

One reason is that the whaling ship is officially engaged not in seeking happiness or heavenly cities, but in a search for wealth. The profits gained are divided into "lays," each in the amount considered warranted by the contribution of a particular member of the crew. The worth of the individual is defined in monetary terms rather than in terms of "divine equality." This makes it as difficult to build a community on board as it is to create a truly "common" school in a society stratified by wealth.

The guiding will on the *Pequod* is that of Captain Ahab, who has been "in colleges" and among cannibals as well. He is seamed, scarred, "dismasted," with an "unsurrendering wilfulness" in his glance and "a crucifixion in his face." Fallible, driven, he seems kingly to his men; he projects himself as a realized personality. His completeness may, in fact, find expression in the inclusiveness of his fragmented crew, the agglomeration ranging from the inscrutable Fedallah, through the natives at their various stages of instinctive power, to the frivolous Flask, the easygoing Stubb, and the pious, responsible Starbuck in whose eyes the Captain can see his own young wife, his child, his leeward home.

Captain Ahab, who may be the ultimate exemplar of self-

reliance, is intent on exerting, without restraint, his free and informed will; this makes him "disintegrative" in his effect. He
wins the frantic loyalty of the crew by offering a gold doubloon
to the first who sights the White Whale. "There is something ever
egotistical . . . ," he muses, engaging individual anger, greed, and
will in such a way that the men voluntarily risk their lives for a
cause that is his alone. They find no "delight" in doing so, for
they are not patriots of God. Nor are they their own inexorable
selves.

In spite of what Ahab's individualism does to his men, Ishmael
is drawn to the Captain from the beginning, fascinated by his
legend, filled with compassion and awe. The "grim aspect" of the
old man affects him. So do his fortitude and "all the nameless
regal overbearing dignity of some mighty woe." Ishmael, sharing
some of his isolation, recognizes that the Captain has plunged
deeper and soared higher than ordinary men, that he may be the
incarnation of the individualist ideal.

But he also discovers that to be as Captain Ahab is requires
the drying up of the "milk and sperm of kindness." When Ishmael
works with his mates at squeezing the lumps of cooled sperma-
ceti into fluid, he sometimes squeezes his fellow laborers' hands
by mistake. When he does so, a kind of "insanity" comes over
him, suggestive of Transcendentalist fantasies of universal communion ("let us all squeeze ourselves into each other. . . ."). Ishmael knows this is excessive, a madness countering Ahab's and
exposing it. He knows, too, that the only realizable dreams of
communion are those modest ones which link an individual's
happiness to particulars, not universals—"the wife, the heart, the
bed, the table, the saddle, the fire-side, the country. . . ." Similarly, the only realizable dreams of self-fulfillment are the limited
and conditional ones, not the dream of imposing one's will upon
the ultimate.

This too holds relevance for the shaping of the democratic
character—outside and within the school. Individuality must be
enriched with an occasional "squeeze of the hand." Personality
must seek enlargement, a fullness of being that includes the

moderation of a Starbuck, the gay acquiescence of a Stubb, the ability of a Flask to "clinch tight," the vitality of a Daggoo, and the dependence of little Pip.

There remains the crucial obligation of the school: to teach children to think, to make knowledge available to them; and the theme of knowing—and the knowable—is another theme fundamental to *Moby-Dick*. On the one hand, the treatment of it evokes the thrust of a country where knowledge was power—power over men and over things. On the other hand, Transcendentalist quests for "higher," purer truths are summoned up, the scholarship that meant penetration of the "veil."

Captain Ahab, who is the exemplar of self-sufficiency, feels justified in exploiting the minds and wills of his crewmen to attain his end. Like the American businessman and speculator, he values knowledge not for its own sake, but for the sake of mastery. (He must not only seek out—he must also destroy the White Whale.) And, like those who saw the schools as merely training grounds for factories, he links the education of his crew to each crew member's vocation, to his duty to the ship or to whaling itself. The men are sailing with him on his voyage toward the ultimate; but all he thinks they need to know is their work. ("It's a partnership," he says about the blacksmith; "he supplies the muscle part.")

But, in his other dimension, Ahab is Emerson's "Man Thinking," the man who trusts his own judgment utterly and permits his intuitions to guide him where they will. Like the Transcendentalist, the Captain takes for granted his ability to push beyond sense experience, to contradict it if he likes. When he throws away his sextant and his compass, he is finally rejecting all the limitations empiricism imposes upon a man. There are no limits after that, no prohibitions against tearing aside the "pasteboard masks" disguising the ultimate, "some unknown but still reasoning thing." Because he has lost his leg, because he is so intellectually proud, he is convinced he sees an "intangible malignity" hanging behind all things, and he identifies it with the White Whale. To prove himself, he must seek vengeance, break through the "wall" Moby-Dick represents, the wall that hems him (and other human beings) in. He converts the Transcendental view, therefore, into a kind of demonism, even as he retains its mysticism and belief in a Being beyond. But now the Transcendent is no longer something luminous, no longer an Oversoul. It is an "inscrutable thing" which Ahab hates; "and be the white whale agent, or be the white whale principal, I will wreak that hatred on him."

The excessiveness of the acquisitive, then, merges in Ahab with the terrible assurance of untested private knowledge; the need for limitation and control again comes clear. It is Ishmael's consciousness that frames the whole, and it is Ishmael who represents the demand that knowledge be validated in a public human world, a world of concretes and actualities. There are moments when he is tempted by Ahab's example, but he does not lose touch with the empirical domain, with experience, or with fact. When he teeters on the masthead like some "sunken-eyed young Platonist," he is aware of the dangers of reverie and abstraction, of the fact that he may lose his balance and disappear in the "Descartian vortices" below.

He tells himself that he must stay interested in the work of the ship and close to his comrades to guard against the feeling of meaninglessness that comes from staring at the sea. He must understand the dangers, too, of the "cetological" concern, with its wild assortment of myths, classifications, generalizations about whaling. Ishmael must know enough to know that inquiry has a terminal point—"the whiteness of the whale."

There is a message here for modern men, especially for those caught up in the sciences, in dreams of "intellectual excellence" and advancing expertise. No matter who the individual is, no matter what his capacity, Ishmael is saying, one must allow one's senses to remain open—one's free imagination, one's heart—and when one has reached the point where the extremes meet, one must stand back at the sight of the "nameless things," the appalling "colorless, all-color" of that which cannot be known.

Only in this manner can a democratic school which is dedicated to knowing fulfill itself. Only with wholeness can there be the "democratic dignity" that is not "the dignity of kings and robes, but that abounding dignity which has no robed investiture." Like Walt Whitman, Melville went on: "Thou shalt see it shining in the arm that wields a pick or drives a spike; that democratic dignity which, on all hands, radiates without end from God." And then he spoke of the crucial value of the common school—equality, and of the "high qualities" to be ascribed to "meanest mariners, and renegades and castaways" by a democratic God who did "pick up Andrew Jackson from the pebbles" to raise him high.

This is the ideal; but, given the nature of the undertaking, the ideal appears unattainable. Ishmael survives, the only one "escaped alone to tell. . . ." He is held up by Queequeg's coffin, which was buoyant enough to spring from the "vital centre" of the whirlpool created by the sinking *Pequod*. He is picked up by the *Rachel*, whose captain still seeks his little boy, lost with a missing whaleboat for which Ahab had refused to be concerned. Ishmael has been narrator and witness, but it has not been his function to be the hero or to save the ship and realize the crew's equality.

Screens of ambiguity are raised, but dimensions of American life which most people never see have been revealed. Yet to refuse to see them is a form of "bachelorism," a denial of "blackness," paradox, and limitation. This may be as inimical to the cause of human fulfillment as the willfulness of powerful men—in a school as well as at sea.

The public's rejection of *Moby-Dick* when it was published is itself a commentary on the American need for optimism. Even Melville's former readers turned away from the image of the vortex whirling the *Pequod*, the crewmen, and the whaleboats out of sight—and of Captain Ahab "shot out of the boat" when caught by the line of his harpoon. The genteel and sentimental stories of the 1850s were preferable to this; so were the dime novels of the age. But the long obliteration of the work and its reappearance in the 1920s make it more rather than less important as a perspective for contemporary minds. It is in recent years that it has become a classic; our twentieth-century experience has made it difficult to deny.

This is largely true of the other tales Melville wrote in the 1850s (before his thirty-year retirement from literature) since these, too, are tales of fundamental questioning. There is his description of young girls chained to machines in a New England paper mill in "The Paradise of Bachelors and the Tartarus of Maids." There are "Bartleby the Scrivener" and "Benito Cereno." Also there is *The Confidence-Man*, in which the stranger on the riverboat may embody dishonesties and frauds implicit in our own affluent world. (Or he may embody "confidence" in another sense—as the innocently trusting attitude associated with "bachelorism.") Readers of tales like these are forced to wonder whether man can ever live without deception and illusion— whether individual affirmation can be reconciled with concern for others, whether justice is possible in a world committed to gain. Those involved with American schools may be left with diminished confidence in their assured success, which may, after all, be just as well. It may be better simply to do one's work well day after day, to try to see through various perspectives—and, now and then, to squeeze some co-worker's hand.

Moderation of this sort was strange to articulate Americans in the days before the Civil War. In the 1850s, the South was alive with melodramatic gestures in defense of the "peculiar institution," as the yeoman majority cast their lot with the slave-holding minority and began justifying slavery as the means of protecting the white man's status in the world. Inevitably, spokesmen for the North began reacting with their own elaborate indictments and justifications. Abolitionism, long the property of a militant, idealistic cult of angry men, became part of a general commitment to "liberty." It became one of the planks in programs calling for free land, high tariffs, and the extension of laissez faire. Horace Greeley and Abraham Lincoln, for example, were typical when they talked for the cause of "free labor" in opposition to the Kansas-Nebraska Act, which was intended to allow slavery, by local option, to exist in portions of the new territories.

Few people, however, were concerning themselves with the conditions under which free labor was being carried on. Few were equipped to think seriously about any aspect of the plight of ordinary working people where laissez-faire policies prevailed. In a Union about to be split apart by war, choirs of voices sang hymns to a freedom valuable for its own sake. No one was able to say clearly what freedom would be *for* or what emancipated Americans were to be.

Prophets were needed, prophets of communion for a silent *en masse*. Teachers were needed to enlighten the autonomous ones and the willful ones, to make some moderate fulfillment possible for those doing the ordinary jobs on a ship still endangered by "vortices" and white whales.

9

THE SONGS OF SELFHOOD
En Masse *and the Ideal*

If a sense of the irreconcilable led Melville to so many incommensurables, a desire for connection and absorption led Walt Whitman in search of the One. He, too, grew up in a pluralist world, "full to completion and varied." Born on a Long Island farm, he was brought to Brooklyn as a child and spent most of his early life across the river from the streaming city. It was the city toward which he would be repeatedly drawn, about which he would write newspaper stories and long chains of poems, through the streets of which he would wander endlessly and drink in the life of the crowds.

He did not go to sea as Melville did; but he was preoccupied with rivers and the ocean, with "the cradle endlessly rocking," with the surge and flow in which he found analogues for life, immortality, and time. For years a newspaper editor, reporter, typesetter, city man, he described himself as a "kosmos" in his first edition of *Leaves of Grass*, the center of "the converging objects of the universe," confident that he could interpret in his own fashion "what the writing means."

He began doing so in 1855, when the first of many *Leaves of Grass* appeared. The ideas and rhythms in the book had been shaped and orchestrated in the twenty years preceding the first publication. He had funneled all his experiences into the poetry: swimming off Paumanok, working with machines and tools, voyaging down the Mississippi, riding the Brooklyn ferry, reading the literature of the past. The immediate stimulus for putting it all down was in Whitman's troubled response to the Mexican War and his perception that the Civil War was soon to begin.

He reacted as would-be prophet, teacher, and seer. He saw "perverse maleficence" in the land, "bawling and blowing office-holders, office-seekers, pimps, malignants, conspirators, murderers, and fancy men." He was aware, as Horace Mann had been, of depravity, dissipation, narrow-mindedness. But he believed that the land was capable of producing an ideal democratic man—that indeed such a man was already latent in the mass, in the "average." His purpose was to summon him forth, to teach the people to release the ideal form they bore within them, to force them to shake off the "contemptible dreams" which prevented them from becoming free and exuberant selves.

Whitman had been an enthusiast of education all his life. In 1846, he had written in the *Brooklyn Daily Eagle* that "American liberality is shown not in matters of vain and childish display—not in baubles and gewgaws, and robes of state, and gilding and satin-cushioned carriages for officers of state—but in munificent grants for the support of Free Schools. . . ."

His philosophy of education was, however, closer to Bronson Alcott's than to Horace Mann's. He espoused the cause of free and well-rounded development in a lively, benevolent atmosphere. For a brief period, he did some teaching and, while in the schools, had bitterly opposed the use of physical punishment and the prisonlike surroundings which caused education to be "hated and shunned." He had written a story, "Death in the School Room," as a public protest against the sadism in the Lancastrian schools. As he was to write much later, two decades after the first *Leaves of Grass*, the schools held "stores of mystic meaning":

Only a lot of boys and girls?
Only the tiresome spelling, writing, ciphering classes?
Only a public school?

Ah more, infinitely more. . . .

It was with somewhat the same feeling that he addressed his readers as his "eleves"—his students. It was as a teacher that he affirmed himself in his physical and spiritual vitality—"Turbulent, fleshly, sensual, eating, drinking, and breeding," embracing all the things of the earth. This was his object lesson: "Myself" as an emblem and embodiment of America, "dazzling and tremendous as the sun," attaining new identities through friendship, "an encloser of things to be."

Nourished by Transcendentalism, he had moved beyond it into a pantheistic idealism which viewed the entire universe as alive with immanent Spirit. All things in nature, he thought, were continuous and fluid. There was a great tidal movement throughout the cosmos which made life continuous with death, men continuous with nature, each human being continuous with each blade of grass. "A child said What is the grass? fetching it to me with full hands. . . ."

> . . . I guess it is a uniform hieroglyphic,
> And it means, Sprouting alike in broad zones and narrow
>   zones,
> Growing among black folks as among white. . . .

Whitman's view of "Personality" was a function of his conception of continuities. It signified the full development of the "Person," which was the world spirit as contained within the individual, the potency that made each living being one with the creative energies flowing in and through his fellow men and everything there was. To be educated, to achieve a personality was, for the poet, to move outward, to enter into others. In America, where there were multitudes, it was to link hands in the *en masse*.

> I do not call one greater and one smaller,
> That which fills its period and place is equal to any.

The "divine average" became a source of potency for anyone who would enter in and allow the "many long dumb voices" to sound through him.

Full of vitality and potentiality as they were, the common

people, Whitman believed, would give birth to the ideal person. He would be one who did not "sweat and whine" about his condition, or discuss his duty to God. He would be interested in everything the people were interested in. He would be able to swim boldly against "the dazzle of light," to embark at any moment on a "perpetual journey" down a forever-open road. He would be the kind who loved and fondled his comrades unashamedly, but who realized that he himself would have to find the answers to his questions. And he would understand that "not anyone else can travel that road for you, You must travel it for yourself."

Such a man, however, could only appear if young people were permitted to express themselves and affirm themselves. Whitman resisted the notion that the school ought to teach each pupil "self-control" and the conception of the school as barrier against passion, or what Horace Mann called "anarchy." Whitman's explorations of "average spiritual manhood" led him to throw down a gauntlet to the McGuffey tradition and the tight moralism binding the schools. Happy men, he believed (as Thoreau did), required no teaching in order to be good. The obstacle was to be found not in disobedience or nonconformity, but in poverty and degradation. These, the poet insisted, were what caused intemperance, crime, and misery, not the depravity of man. Once social inequities were removed, once men were no longer "demented with the mania of owning," once the plain people were no longer doomed to lives of "sweating, ploughing, thrashing and then the chaff for payment receiving," moral behavior would be wholly natural.

In order to expose the evils of prurience, repression, and guilt, he risked offending his audiences with descriptions of the joys of sexuality. No one before had rebelled against the traditional ethic by so openly doting upon himself, worshiping "the spread of my own body," finding it "luscious," reaching out for unashamed contact as "mate and companion," procreant lover of mankind. His posture of acceptance and affirmation was chosen as a means of liberating people from their fears, their denials of their wholly natural selves.

What blurt is this about virtue and about vice?
Evil propels me and reform of evil propels me, I stand
    indifferent,
My gait is no fault-finder's or rejecter's gait;
I moisten the roots of all that is grown.

Again, he was attempting to teach common men to be uncommon, to be as encompassing as "Walt Whitman, liberal and
lusty as Nature. . . ." He identified, while doing so, with the
process of idealizing the common man in dime novels, stories of
the West, and the growing folklore of giants like Paul Bunyan
and Pecos Bill. The average American, as he saw him, could be
as grand and godlike as an Ahab; but, at once, he could be wed
to life by remaining part of the *en masse*.

He would be robust, open to the "love of comrades"; he would
find dignity and pride in work. In "Song of Myself," he wrote that
"there is no trade or employment but the young man following it
may become a hero. . . ." But work was not to be a form of slavery, or a penance, or a punishment. He heard singing where others thought men mute:

I hear America singing, the varied carols I hear,
Those of mechanics, each one singing his as it should be
    blithe and strong,
The carpenter singing his as he measures his plank or beam,
The mason singing his as he makes ready for work, or leaves
    off work,
The boatman singing what belongs to him in his boat, the
    deck-hand singing on the steamboat deck,
The shoemaker singing as he sits on his bench, the hatter
    singing as he stands,
The woodcutter's song, the ploughboy's on his way in the
    morning, or at noon intermission or at sundown. . . .

The songs would be expressive of the singers, but they would not
be sung to the beat of each one's particular drum. Whitman saw

people marching together; he saw himself coming with his "cor-
nets and drums" to play music all could move to—*en masse*.

The separate voices would not be absorbed, however. There
was a place for each one's, just as there was a place for each blade
of grass. But men had to keep their feet on the ground and perceive the continuities among them to realize that "a leaf of grass
is no less than the journey-work of the stars" and that "all truths
wait in all things. . . ." There were times when Whitman raised
cheers for "positive science," for useful facts gained at all levels
of understanding; but there were other times when he seemed to
trust the validity of simple people's judgments more than any
scholarship. "Logic and sermons," he wrote, "never convince."
Nor, in certain moods, did he find science convincing. Hearing
"the learn'd astronomer," he described himself as growing tired
of "the proofs, the figures," he was asked to contemplate, "the
charts and diagrams. . . ." So he wandered off alone "in the mystical moist night-air." While the astronomer lectured inside, he
"look'd up in perfect silence at the stars."

Some of this, perhaps, was due to his desire to give his hearers
confidence in their own perceptions. He was telling them to remain *within* experience, to say "I accept Reality and dare not
question it." An individual's "Reality" was what he was equipped
to see from his vantage point in life. Attempting to teach, to
arouse, Whitman was asking that each person open himself to a
manifold of sensations—enlarge himself and his reality.

This was one reason for his affirmation of the city, an affirmation
rare among artists of the time. He was able to find "mast-hemmed
Manhattan" a source of wonder. He was able to celebrate the stir
of shipping and commerce in the harbor, to find the fires of
foundry chimneys beautiful and their smoke "a necessary film."
To encompass what there was to begin to understand it, to deal
with it. The democratic hero Whitman had in mind was to be
healthy enough to appropriate all that existed in American life.

Reaching out in so many directions, the poet inevitably came
in contact with a number of the age's intellectual tendencies. He
did not always apprehend them rationally; he often registered

their effects in a feeling-tone or a mood. But he was open to a good many currents of thought, and their mark was left on his work. Easiest to identify is the connection between some of his ideas and certain innovations in education at the time; but this is not because of clear lines of influence. Again, it is due to a similarity of concern or mood.

The similarity is clearest when the kindergarten movement is recalled, and the German emigrés who brought it to the United States. Whitman was in several ways akin to Francis Wayland Parker, who began, in the 1870s, to apply insights adapted from the kindergarten movement to the primary grades in the Quincy, Massachusetts, schools. Already preparing for what would be called the "New Education," Parker was Whitmanesque when he enjoined his teachers to concentrate on the growing child, to cultivate the sort of self-realization which "consists in improving the condition of mankind through personal effort." Like Whitman, he stressed correlations and continuities in his subject matter; "genuine physical contact" with the world of work and trade; knowledge for the sake of "the best life" rather than for power, prominence, or gain.

Whitman's writings were also tributary to wider and more complex streams of thought, several of which were to empty into a slow-moving river of educational theory after the Civil War. The source of many of these was in philosophical idealism, notably the idealism of the Transcendentalists which had so deeply influenced Whitman in his youth.

Among the most important streams was that of Kantian idealism, from which Transcendentalism had borrowed a number of its central themes. According to Immanuel Kant, whatever order there was, whatever meanings were to be found in the physical world, were fabricated by the human mind. The mind was equipped with certain rational categories through which understanding took place; and it was by means of these categories (or patterns, or "schema,") that sensory experiences were organized into the objective, orderly, determinist system described by science as "the external world."

Although they appreciated the notion of the mind's creative and legislative capacity, the Transcendentalists tended to be less concerned than Kant had been with "pure reason" and its functions. They responded most of all to the idea that human beings could not rationally penetrate the "phenomenal" realm of sensory experience and arrive at the "thing-in-itself," from which sensations derived. They developed this idea into their own conception of the "veil" which intuitions might break through. And they attempted to combine their conception with Kant's view of "practical reason," which, in the ethical dimension of life, enabled man to know immediately and absolutely the principles of right and duty. It was in this dimension that the human being, as Kant conceived him, knew himself to be possessed of free will and the apprehension of God.

Kant concentrated, therefore, on cultivating rationality, so that the human being might grow out of barbarism and become "human" enough (or rational enough) to intuit the right—to know his duty. The Transcendentalists, in contrast, put their main stress on freedom, on an almost mystical "leap," not toward knowledge of a "categorical imperative," but toward union with the Oversoul. Kant's vision of a "Kingdom of Ends," governed by rationally apprehended moral law, was superseded by a vision of man as "transparent eyeball," or, as Emerson put it, "part or particle of God."

There is irony in the fact that Kantianism eventually exerted an influence on American education in a way neither a Transcendentalist nor a Whitman would approve. The pedagogical "science" of the German philosopher Johann Friedrich Herbart, who followed Kant as professor of philosophy at Königsberg, was adapted to the American situation by the American Herbartians Charles and Frank McMurry and Charles De Garmo in the 1890s. Developing what they conceived to be a wholly "rational" approach to teaching, they explored in detail the doctrine of "interest," the potential contributions to character building to be found in literature and history, and the "five-step" method of instruction (recollection, presentation, comparison, generalization, application). Their end-in-view, reminiscent of Kant, was the training of a "good will" in every child, and thus the shaping of "good character."

For all its contributions to the theoretical study of education, Herbartianism was formal and controlling in its implications for practice. Whitman would have found it permeated by a commitment to moral "blurt"; the Transcendentalists would have rejected its didacticism, its intellectualism.

In any case, even before the Civil War, a fresh tide of idealism had moved in from Germany, more suggestive and, in time, more influential than Kantianism in its American guise. This was the idealism of Georg W. F. Hegel, an abstract of which came by chance to Whitman's attention when he was in need of sanction for his own departures from Transcendentalism. There is some doubt that he fully understood what was involved in Hegelianism, but he declared himself an advocate and said he had found a "fusing explanation" in it, an understanding of the varieties in life and time as "different steps or links in the endless process of creative thought. . . ."

He said, too, that he discovered a justification for American democracy in Hegelianism. In a poem called "Roaming in Thought" (written "after reading Hegel") he wrote:

> Roaming in thought over the Universe, I
> saw the little that is Good steadily
> hastening towards immortality,
>   And the vast all that is call'd Evil I
> saw hastening to merge itself and become
> lost and dead.

This was a very free rendering of Hegel's conception of an external reality always in the process of becoming, or of his notion of a "World-Spirit" ascending dialectically in history toward a final synthesis of all contending contraries in creation—a final consummation in the Absolute, the Mind of God.

Whitman probably did not see that, for Hegel, reality was

thought objectified, that nature itself was "God thinking," that "reason" and "being" were one. What he did see was the possibility of resolving the contradictions and overcoming the dichotomies that had plagued America from the beginning—and were now about to tear her apart. He found in Hegel's idea of the organic interrelatedness of all things a sanction for his own view of continuities pervading the natural and human world. For Hegel, however, the unity and completeness of the whole were identified with the Absolute, which contained all things in its infinite thought. The Absolute—which *was* the totality, the world in its completeness—had become conscious of itself in, and by means of, humankind. This signified, on the one hand, a special uniqueness and dignity in man; on the other, it meant that the laws of human reason were the same as the laws of the universe. What followed was crucial in Hegelianism but alien, in many respects, to Whitman: the real was rational; and whatever was rational was real. Yet the conception of an encompassing Absolute Idea which was the world (and not the creator of it) came very close to the pantheism characteristic of Whitman's view. The difference was that, for Hegel, individuals were organic parts of a developing, *thinking* World-Spirit, each part of which was knowable, because the structure as a whole was analogous with the human mind.

Also, Hegelianism, with its conception of abstract Right and subjective morality clashing and becoming synthesized in objectively existent Ethics, tended to be less open, less potentially creative than Whitman's imagined picture of the real. The Absolute, in fact, was conceived to be embodied objectively in social institutions which reached their ideal culmination in a perfect State. This State was far more important than any individual and the primary source of individual freedom and rationally determined rights.

The effect of this, in the last analysis, was exceedingly conservative. The individual tended to be subsumed, not only under the Absolute but (as a concrete, existing being) under the abstractness of a world become a rational construct, an Idea. This was to become particularly significant in America when it was embodied in one of the most influential schools of thought to appear in the nineteenth century and, at length, to affect the functioning of public schools.

The academic cradle of Hegelianism was, not surprisingly, in Missouri, the state so tragically bifurcated by the Missouri Compromise. There worked William Torrey Harris, who became superintendent of the St. Louis public schools in 1867. Introduced to Hegel's philosophy by a German emigré who saw resemblances between the United States and his own divided country, Harris and a colleague had begun reading, studying, and translating large sections of Hegel's works. In 1867 they launched the *Journal of Speculative Philosophy*, a landmark in the development of "the American scholar," although, because it was explicitly Hegelian in orientation, not what Emerson had originally had in mind. Objecting in their first issue to the perpetuation of the "brittle individualism" which they saw as but an early phase of America's political growth, the editors went on to talk about the next essential phase, in which the individual was to find his freedom "in the realization of the rational conviction which finds expression in established law."

The power of the Hegelians' ideas and personalities was demonstrated a few years later when the elderly Bronson Alcott came to St. Louis to deliver some of his oracular "Orphic sayings." Harris and some of his Hegelian friends attempted to move Alcott into more precise definition of his beliefs, and they succeeded in weaning the old man from his own distinctive "individualism" as well as from his Emersonian attachment to notions like the "Oversoul." One consequence of this was the establishment, by Harris and Alcott, of the Concord Summer School of Philosophy in Massachusetts, which brought together (in transient and somewhat uneasy union) Midwestern and Eastern idealisms.

The career of the Summer School ended in 1889, when Harris was appointed United States Commissioner of Education. In that position, he discovered a vast forum for the propagation of

Hegelian ideas. Although the Bureau of Education in the Department of the Interior was assigned no powers of supervision or control, the Commissioner had many opportunities to perform educational functions of his own. Like Horace Mann in Massachusetts and like Henry Barnard, the first United States Commissioner of Education, Harris made full use of annual reports and lecture assignments in the communication of his pedagogical ideas.

Concerned with a "larger culture" which might enlist the loyalties of American youth, he stressed the necessity for "obedience to what is prescribed by authority." When Harris spoke of authority, he referred to an organic structure of authorities, beginning with the family and ascending through employers and the government to "the divine will, howsoever revealed." For all his intellectual commitment, he put "deportment, or behavior" first in his order of priorities. "Order," he said, was required in every school; "each pupil must be taught to conform his behavior to the general standard and repress all that interferes with the function of the school." The proper performance of each person's duty, he pointed out, would insure the realization of his "higher ideal nature," which was the same as the "true inward self of our fellow men."

Each individual, he said, was to be bound to the great ascending pyramid of civilization by ties of duty, discipline, and rational mastery. Each was to come to understand the skills and knowledge gathered by the human race in the course of history and to raise himself, with their assistance, above the level of barbarism at which he was destined to begin. The educational goal was to be unity with the Absolute. Self-government, compliance with the laws of righteousness and duty, conformity with the *status quo*—none of these was a sufficient justification for a public school, Harris believed. American youth ought to be inducted into a spiritual "establishment" through their schooling. Every individual ought to strive to become an organic part of the encompassing whole. Only then would the public school fulfill its promise.

It would become the agent of reconciliation, the means of effecting a synthesis out of the tension between social order and individual desire.

Academic Hegelianism, then, pursued what may have been its necessary course, once it found an institutional guise. But it was a course far removed from what Walt Whitman had chosen to see. He had discovered sanctions for his own vision in his reading of Hegel's work. The guarantees he thought he found, however, were guarantees of a continuous "Song of Myself." To perceive continuities in nature was not to subordinate the concrete individual, as Whitman saw it; "the endless process of creative thought" was to give rise to life-affirming, unique persons, not to an Absolute made conscious of itself.

Calling for comradeship and communion, Whitman had tried to appropriate wide, grand gestures for the ordinary man, liberated for walking the open road with his fellows, dignified because he was alive and free. Individualism was in no sense a first or lower stage. The true individual was to emerge from the mass as a realization of democracy—the completion of the poem, the justification for the school. The difficulty was that Whitman was defining such ends when individualism, working through industry and finance and even slavery, was threatening to destroy individuality in the *en masse*.

And yet, without such visionary definitions, the school might have been conceived merely as a training ground for faceless men. Without an infatuation with the "self," without a faith in what Melville's Ishmael saw as "that abounding dignity which has no robed investiture," a doctrine like William Torrey Harris' might have avoided all challenge through the heyday of public schools.

The Civil War intervened between *Leaves of Grass* and that heyday, between the wishful application of laissez faire ideas to schools and the appointment of Harris as United States Commissioner. The first responses to war, in both North and South, gave evidence of a need for heroic visions and for a heightened consciousness of the self. "The greatness of the crisis, the Homeric grandeur of the contest," wrote a journalist in 1861, "surrounds and elevates us all." President Lincoln said in 1862 that his Administration would be remembered "in spite of ourselves" because, as he put it, "we cannot escape history." Oliver Wendell Holmes Jr. told of what the experience meant to him and his contemporaries: "It was given to us to learn at the outset that life is a profound and passionate thing." Emerson, summing up at the end of the war, wrote that patriotism had been but "a fire-work, a salute, a serenade for holidays and summer evenings" before the fighting. Now, after all the deaths and the commitment of the people, patriotism had turned out to be real.

This happens to some degree during any war, but the Civil War was a war between Americans. In many respects, the cause was what Shakespeare's Hamlet calls an "eggshell"—not so much the defense of the Union as the defense of what the Union signified: industrial expansion, free labor, cheap land, laissez faire. The values associated with these were suddenly transmuted. No longer did they signify simply the *status quo*, materialism, Trade. They took on, for the moment, a borrowed luster; it became easier to touch, in Melville's words, each "workman's arm with some ethereal light."

It became easier, at least theoretically, to impart a mythic quality to education, devoted as it was to the ends for which the Union fought. But such a quality could not be rationally maintained—nor could the heroic atmosphere of war. In the Gilded Age that lay ahead, the school would be asked to service an increasingly mass society, to meet the needs of expanding industry, to teach young citizens "obedience to what is prescribed by authority."

Would it be possible to "hear America singing" in the emerging, industrial age? Or would Whitman's "Prayer of Columbus" become relevant?

Is it the prophet's thought I speak, or am I raving?
What do I know of life? what of myself?
I know not even my own work past or present. . . .

10

THE PREDICAMENTS OF FREEDOM
The Negro, the Farmer, and Huck Finn

Whitman's "Democratic Vistas" appeared in 1871, six years after Appomattox and the death of Lincoln, the poet's "ideal man." The pamphlet began as a jeremiad for the days of problematic victory:

> I say we had best look our times and lands searchingly in the face, like a physician diagnosing some deep disease. Never was there, perhaps, more hollowness at heart than at present, and here in the United States. Genuine belief seems to have left us. The underlying principles of the States are not honestly believ'd in (for all this hectic glow, and these melodramatic screamings), nor is humanity itself believ'd in. What penetrating eye does not everywhere see through the mask?

The mask was one of exuberance and self-assertion for those economic adventurers untroubled by narrow morality. Gould, Morgan, Fiske, Vanderbilt, and the others surely did not pay heed to the "blurt" Whitman had mocked before the Civil War; and when Andrew Carnegie transformed it into a "Gospel of Wealth," the traditional ethic did little to restrain what Whitman called "the depravity of the business classes," or "respectable as much as unrespectable robbery and scoundrelism."

It seemed, however, that a man had to be an artist, a scholar, or a utopian to penetrate the busy surfaces of Northern post-war life. Writers of acknowledged talent were almost unanimous in their response to what the Republican Party's hegemony was coming to mean. The forms they chose were varied; but Melville, Mark Twain, William Dean Howells, Henry Adams, and others joined Whitman in pointing out what had happened to degrade "American ideals." In New England, the aged Emerson came together with Octavius Brooks Frothingham and other rationalists and freethinkers to form the Free Religious Association, dedicated to the preservation of human dignity, to the eventual foundation of a universal "co-operative union," and to the creation of a "religion of humanity" in the place of restrictive Christianity. Robert Ingersoll began lecturing about a new humanism to be committed to belief in science's potential service to mankind, in human freedom, and in a society made equitable at last, no longer split between "gorged indolence and famished industry." Henry George was soon to be talking "single tax" and a welfare state; Edward Bellamy was soon to write *Looking Backward*, describing a Utopia based on the "Brotherhood of Humanity."

And the educators, the men who spoke for public schools? It is true that they made many statements about the common-school ideal, the need for universal educational opportunity, the need for extending the common school upward until an educational "ladder" was built from the primary grades to the university gates. But there is no evidence of social critique in the postwar years. Educational spokesmen talked as if a moral as well as an economic victory had been forever secured, and the logic of their traditional arguments led them to play increasingly conservative roles. They supported, with scarcely a demurrer, the government's encouragement of railroad-building, industrial expansion, and financial speculation. They did not see—or chose to ignore—what less practical men were calling, in the words of Charles Francis Adams, "organized lawlessness under the forms of law."

The schoolmen's record of dissidence had been generally limited to the cause of abolition; after Emancipation, they saw little cause for unrest. The South's long-standing lack of interest in common schools made it a simple matter for those concerned with public education to identify wholly with the Union and to treat the victories of business and free labor as victories for their schools.

The South, with a class system quite different from that of the North, a deliberately created agrarian "mystique," and a preoccupation with what was seen as the menace of Negro domination, acknowledged few of the arguments for universal schooling. Except for the unique accomplishments of Superintendent Calvin Wiley in North Carolina and a truncated effort to establish free schools in Virginia, no significant effort had ever been made to provide even primary education at public expense.

When certain Northerners—teachers, for example—went to stay in the South, they were sometimes asked to leave town because they were suspected of being antislavery. Carl Degler quotes a newspaper in a South Carolina town, justifying the expulsion of two teachers from the North: "Nothing definite is known of their abolition or insurrectionary sentiments, but being from the North and necessarily imbued with doctrines hostile to our institutions their presence in this section has been obnoxious and at any rate suspicious."

Just before the outbreak of war, a number of Southern newspapers had demanded the censorship of textbooks used in academies. Efforts were made to keep Southern college students in institutions near home instead of sending them North. After the war, Henry Barnard indirectly supported those efforts when he asserted that Northern schools had no responsibility for reducing sectional rivalries. It was in a mood of irreconcilability that the educators supported Radical Reconstruction, when the program was chosen over Lincoln's plan for gradual reconciliation. And it was not accidental that Thaddeus Stevens, the champion of the free school in Pennsylvania, became the leader of Radical Reconstructionism.

The 1866 election indicated widespread support for Negro equality, although Negroes were still disenfranchised in many Northern states. When the Southern states refused to ratify the

Fourteenth Amendment, and when they withheld suffrage and equal rights from their Negro citizens, military rule was established in each state until the day when its constitution would be altered and the amendment ratified. There were attacks by the Ku Klux Klan and others upon the Negro population, but the federal government was cautious about intervening and no actual military occupation occurred.

Nevertheless, Negroes were able to vote by tens of thousands, and there were startling electoral victories of Negroes and Radicals during the Reconstruction period. These were due partly to a temporary disenfranchisement of certain whites and partly to the resentful withdrawal of others from all political life. When the Negroes won the minor executive positions allotted to them, or when they took seats in the legislatures, they tended to behave temperately toward white people; in spite of exaggerated reports of barbaric behavior, there is scarcely any evidence of fraud or lawlessness in the efforts they made to win elections and play governmental roles. And, despite the horror tales of "Black Legislatures," the Negroes remained in the minority in all the state assemblies but those of Louisiana and South Carolina, where they were in the majority only for a brief time.

It was in New Orleans, though, and Charleston, that there had been the largest proportion of educated freedmen. This was of the first importance, although contemporary Northern educators said nothing about it, just as no one of them supported South Carolina's innovative effort to provide for integrated schools. (Even in Massachusetts, there were still "separate but equal" facilities for the children of Negroes and whites.)

Before Reconstruction, the only serious efforts to provide public schooling in the defeated South had been made on behalf of white children. It was left to the Freedmen's Bureau to establish elementary and industrial schools for Negro youth. The violence of pre-Reconstruction days had found frequent expression in attacks on those schools, but the commitment to education was strong enough to permit thousands of them to survive. Once the Reconstruction state governments were formed, dual public

school systems were established with provisions for eventual admission of all children, and they were maintained in many areas
after Reconstruction came to a halt in 1877. Economic arguments for literate workingmen were seeping into the South by
then and it seemed for a while as if Southerners were becoming
accustomed to the idea of free schooling, for Negroes as well as
for whites.

For several years after 1877, in fact, there was reason for hop-
ing that the old hatreds and fears would soon abate. Negroes were
allowed to retain their suffrage rights. Here and there people were
talking of the wastefulness of a dual school system, sometimes
agreeing with the New York editor who said segregated schooling was "unchristian and bad." Spokesmen for the public schools
confined their remarks to comments on the importance of education in preventing the return of slavery. In official capacities,
they said nothing about integrating the schools or about equal
opportunity.

Then, suddenly, it was too late. The era of acquiescence ended
in the South, as if it had never been. Abolitionist and humanitarian hopes were quashed by a decision handed down by the
Supreme Court in 1883. It dealt with certain civil rights cases
which had arisen in connection with efforts to enforce the Fourteenth Amendment. Some concerned the Negroes' right to free
access to public accommodations; others had to do with the federal government's role in protecting Negro rights. The decision
restored to the states the responsibility for race relations and to
the municipalities the right to define relevant codes.

And then it all began: the reiteration of the "states' rights"
theme; segregation ordinances and the invention of "Jim Crow"
restrictions; devices to prevent Negroes from voting; Ku Klux
Klan night rides and talk of "white supremacy"; the Convict
Lease System, chain gangs, and the rest. Vann Woodward quotes
a statement made at the Mississippi Constitutional Convention
in 1890 on "the policy of crushing out the manhood of Negro citizens. . . ." Yet the Northern schoolmen, so long concerned with
what they had termed "equality," seemed (as Whitman put it) af-

flicted with "hollowness of heart." They continued working to extend public school systems through the South; but, although they talked about the significance of emancipation, they were unable to respond to the individual Negro who had been set free—the living human creature in his uniqueness and his need. They helped (innocently, perhaps) to make the Negro "invisible" in the sense in which Ralph Ellison uses the word.

"You ache," Ellison's hero says in *Invisible Man*, "with the need to convince yourself that you do exist in the real world, that you're a part of all the sound and anguish. . . ." It was that way in the 1880s; it is that way now. And a variety of re-enactments are taking place, reminiscent of what was happening eighty years ago. Not only are Negro men and women demanding recognition as persons, the white American, too, can be seen striving to affirm himself as a whole and significant person again, free to choose an identity. In the 1880s the predicament of the emancipated slaves put American idealism to a dreadful test, one only a few chose to confront. Today the movement for civil rights has affected thousands of white people, a challenge to their sense of themselves as persons as well as to their conception of democracy.

In the last century, like today, it was possible, as Whitman said, "to wash the gum from your eyes." There was a New Orleans newspaperman named George Washington Cable, who returned from fighting with the Confederate Army to find himself rejecting the segregationist cause. During Reconstruction the schools were momentarily integrated in New Orleans; he was able to see classes taught by Negro and white teachers, to see "both races standing in the same classes and giving each other peaceable, friendly, and effective competition. . . ."

When his opinions cost him his job, Cable arraigned by letter some students whose protests had prevented the hiring of a French mulatto mathematics teacher in 1875 and whose brutalities had forced some Negro girls out of school. He expressed his outrage at the holding of a mass meeting to protest integrated schools, and in 1883 he exposed the chain gang in "The Freedman's Case in Equity," published in a Northern magazine.

Cable wrote works of fiction later on, novels on miscegenation, the alienation of the mulatto, the grotesque cruelties of Southern gentlefolk. He also lectured on platforms across the country, telling people in the North and West about the bigotries of the South as they bore upon the schools. Audiences listened; the educators, in some sense most concerned, did nothing.

The National Education Association had had several opportunities to challenge educational inequalities in the South. One of the most potent challenges was embodied in the Hoar Bill, which would have enabled the federal government to intervene in cases of state delinquency in providing education for the young. Because the bill called for the sending of inspectors into local districts, it might have insured remedial action in the case of injustices like those Cable described.

The public schoolmen, however, joined the Catholic Church in opposing the bill, as they had opposed and would oppose all attempts to establish common standards for the nation's schools. Their arguments were grounded in their objections to centralization and in a conception of republicanism which excluded any element of "uniformity." Their neglect of the special dangers facing the Negro child is underlined by the alternatives they proposed between 1870 and 1890: every proposal focused on aid to local districts, even in the most prejudiced areas of the South.

Post-Reconstruction schooling for the Negroes, then, became almost wholly dependent on philanthropy and private effort. The Peabody and then the Slater funds were created, to be used to stimulate selected local schools to provide adequate "intellectual, moral, or industrial" training in destitute areas of the South, most of which were populated by Negroes. Something, in any event, was salvaged for Negro youth in school districts profiting from the funds; much was done to promote teacher education. And, although that had not been the original intention, the funds helped guarantee the survival of many Southern district schools.

Philanthropy was also responsible for the spread of industrial and workshop training for Negro youth. The interest in "practical" education stemmed from an old Protestant tradition, but it was helped immeasurably by the rationale defined by Booker T. Washington, ex-slave, prophet of expediency and submission. As Washington saw it, the Southern Negro, handicapped as he was, would benefit by accepting segregation and concentrating on self-improvement. This meant devotion to learning the skills that could advance him economically in a "realistic" sphere. Washington became the founder of Tuskegee Institute, which for many years perpetuated his views and gave them status in the white domain. They aroused opposition, however, among Negro scholars like W. E. B. Du Bois; and clearly, they effected what Ellison's hero calls "a more efficient binding" into attitudes of inferiority.

Yet, in a speech at the Atlanta trade fair in 1895, Washington talked in terms startlingly similar to those used by public schoolmen when he spoke of glorifying life's "common occupations" and distinguishing between "the ornamental gewgaws of life and the useful." There was, he said, "as much dignity in tilling a field as in writing a poem," and he warned against an "artificial forcing" of the Negro. The prime necessity, he asserted, was "to earn a dollar" before undertaking anything else. For his own reasons, then, Washington made himself part of the movement that was demanding education for efficiency and utility—education that would equip the mass of people to function adequately in an industrialized world.

In the philosophical dimension, William Torrey Harris had been developing a worldview that would sanction just such educational concerns. In the realm of sociology, there were numerous devotees of the British thinker Herbert Spencer, who had constructed what was believed to be a systematic science of social evolution based on Darwinian principles. He had begun spelling out some of its implications for education before the Civil War, and they had turned out to be congruent at many points with the ideas of those who saw the schools as agencies of adaptation, as places where children were trained in the "common occupations" suitable to their time.

Spencer had completed his essays on education in 1859, essays which began with the query "What knowledge is of most worth?" That was the year in which Horace Mann died (after serving for six years as President of Antioch College) and the year in which John Dewey was born in Burlington, Vermont. It was also the year of publication of Charles Darwin's *On the Origin of Species*, which was to cause a ferment in the sciences and theology, and was soon to move educators in many countries toward a new concern for development and adaptation in the midst of change.

Trained as an engineer, Spencer reached maturity in the milieu in which Darwin worked—and in which the ideas of British liberalism and utilitarianism were churning in a crucible of scientific speculation. Dogmatic and individualistic, Spencer was certain he had the answers to questions in the range of scientific fields. He built his approach to education on the absolutist premise, "Science is of most worth." Science meant specific practical information, specifically relevant to the activities of life: those which ministered to self-preservation; those having to do with the rearing of children, with maintaining proper social and political relationships, and with making use of leisure time. Education, he said, ought to prepare children for "complete living"; this meant that it ought to make them knowledgeable and therefore effectual in the major activities he had defined.

Spencer objected to trivial, impractical education, to "elegance," ornament, and abstraction. He placed the classical and literary studies last in his proposed curriculum. Moral education, as he saw it, was to be carried on through the "discipline of natural consequences," which meant a discipline by which each child was made to "pay" for each wrongdoing, with the penalty following directly as cause followed effect.

American readers found much that was familiar and reassuring in what Spencer had said. Social scientist William Graham Sumner gave wide currency to Spencerian doctrines in the academic world. In spite of his own considerable skepticism respecting American public schools, Sumner found sanctions for their existence in some of Spencer's beliefs. The schools could be justified, he said, by the contributions they were capable of making to the maintenance of public order. But it would be evolution, not education, which would bring progress about by selecting those most fit to prosper and survive.

All this suggested to conservative schoolmen a number of imperatives for teaching in the cities and company towns. The first requirement was stability and discipline wherever workers were needed for the booming factories. School administrators tended to identify with business interests, and it was not difficult for them to define "fitness" and "adaptation" as pedagogical "goods."

It was somewhat different where farmers' children were concerned. Educators neglected the plight of those on the "middle border" and on the far frontiers; their continuing lack of interest in the rural schools made their dedication to industrial development appear altogether single-minded. The industrial magnates themselves had lost sympathy with the idea of maintaining the West as a "safety valve" for hard-pressed workers during hard times. For their own good reasons, they frowned on attempts to improve the quality of rural life. They were not yet worried about possibilities of serious agrarian unrest—in spite of dust storms and indebtedness which made conditions worse each year.

Perhaps out of loyalty, perhaps out of intellectualist bias, the educational leaders ignored opportunities provided by the Morrill Act of 1862, which called for land grants to make possible the establishment of agricultural and mechanical colleges and institutes. Indeed, they exerted a minimum of pressure for the extension of the free school systems in the Western and Midwestern states. Given such lack of encouragement and the long-time rural suspicion of "book-larnin'," country schooling developed on an abysmally low level, and gains in literacy lagged far behind the East's.

The curriculum in the one-room country schoolhouses, as Edward Eggleston and Hamlin Garland were to make clear, was as abstract and sterile as the curriculum in the city schools. Here, however, the ill-trained teachers' stress on "mental discipline," docility, and the virtues and graces thought essential for a genteel urban life made what was taught seem wholly irrelevant to country children. There seemed to be no classroom knowledge of recognizable "worth." It was meaningless in the extreme.

In a time when few of the country's orators were articulating the values of rural existence, the sense of futility and meaninglessness began to trouble many of those who had been reared in awareness of what Henry Nash Smith has named "the myth of the Garden." The "Garden" was the Western place of possibility and beginning—the prairie, the mountain, the open plain. It was the Promised Land where there were always new opportunities for those willing to "pack up and strike westward," as Horace Greeley had said. Now, in the 1880s and 1890s, people were losing their faith in both promise and actuality, and there was something about the empty prattle in their schoolrooms that helped to increase the irrelevance of the myth.

There had been, of course, a great increase in Western migration in the days after the war; but for all the promise of the Homestead Act, the little men in need of a "safety valve" were with increasing frequency left behind. The "iron horse" outraced them; speculators outmaneuvered them—money-men like Morgan and Gould, franchise-seekers like Vanderbilt, adventurers like Rockefeller, all the clerks and banks and shopkeepers who were squeezing small farmers into dependence and tight-fisted impecuniousness.

Inevitably, agrarian loyalties fragmented. It was a time when great hearty businessmen and financiers were, like Colonel Sellers in Mark Twain's and Warner's *The Gilded Age*, dreaming of "whole Atlantic oceans of cash . . . , gulfs and bays thrown in." They were the ones pursuing white whales, living out the enactments of the Dream. Yet the true legatees of the original promise were the people on the plains and prairies, the small-town people of the dry places, washed up on the shores.

Mark Twain, born Samuel L. Clemens in 1835, encompassed the movement outward—the expectations, hungers, laughs, losses, and tears. He enacted it as he lived his life in the open places, on the rivers and oceans, in printing houses, mines, and gambling halls. Then, feeling stifled by comfort and success, he looked backward through the paned glass of a house in Hartford, Connecticut, and wrote his major works. The masterwork deals with the education of an American—with a youngster's initiation into a way of life the author knew was doomed to disappear.

Mark Twain had looked hard at America since leaving the town where he was born in divided, slave-holding Missouri. He had worked in cities; like Melville, he had stood often at a helm, in his case the helm of a Mississippi steamboat where, as apprentice pilot, he had learned to steer "through snags and blind reefs," to avoid sunken wrecks, to keep afloat in a "murky waste of water."

The Adventures of Huckleberry Finn was begun a decade before its publication in 1884. The tale opens with an account of children's games in village darkness and with Huck's "long think" about rewards and punishments, about the futility of prayer. Huck knows he is an outsider and is aware of being "kind of lowdown and ornery." He has no hope of the widow's kindly God adopting him; and he thinks that Tom Sawyer's "lies" about heroism, genies, elephants are equally irrelevant, with "all the marks of a Sunday-school."

Miss Watson and the Widow Douglas have been trying to "sivilize" or educate him, but Huck can only sweat and fidget under their ministrations and feel "all cramped up." When his Pap comes and takes him away from civilization to the cabin across the river, he finds it "lazy and jolly" living in the woods, except for Pap's "cowhide" control. When, at length, he fixes things to make his father think he has been murdered, he starts off on a journey down the river by himself. But as soon as he finds an island he can claim as his own, he settles down as if he has come home.

Feeling himself a child of nature, he constructs a natural order of his own. It is an order opposed to the widow's constricting culture and to Tom Sawyer's fantasies as well. Within its boundaries,

Huck is wholly competent: he knows how to make a fire, steer a raft, catch fish to be "haggled" open with a saw. He can judge the current of the river, interpret sounds, identify the passing boats; also, he can enter other people's private lives, take other names, play other roles. He is thoroughly adapted to the environment of the wilderness. The trouble is that the wilderness is becoming spoiled, and, when human beings cheat each other there, and kill and steal and feud, he becomes uneasy, scared, often just an irresponsible child.

He re-enacts the American adventure, the movement outward from the settlement; but he cannot build his own natural Heavenly City, as his ancestors thought they could. He cannot, because too many kinds of evil have usurped the riverbanks; it is too late to find the New Jerusalem or any other Promised Land. A frame house is carried past on the flooded stream. It is full of signs of recent habitation, of drinking, too, and gambling—and a naked dead man is lying on the floor. A steamboat is wrecked, "mournful and lonesome" in the river; there is a trio of murderers on board, all soon to drown.

There are, however, the shock and delight of meeting Jim, who has also "lit out"—in his case from slavery. Jim is like a Queequeg, now become a man of righteousness and dignity. He knows how to protect and love; he creates a refuge from a storm, and Huck "wouldn't want to be nowhere else. . . ." When Huck is lost in the fog, Jim weeps for him; and, when Huck tries to fool him and tell him it was a dream, Jim says he ought to be ashamed to do that to a friend whose heart "wuz mos' broke bekase you wuz los'. . . ." Jim's quiet acceptance abruptly makes Huck capable of humility: "I almost kissed *his* foot" to get him to forgive.

Because Jim feels so deeply, because he calls Huck "honey" and his best friend and "ole true Huck," the boy gains the strength to act against his "conscience," actually the conscience of the slave-holding community in which he was schooled. When he discovers that Jim is being hunted, he carefully weighs the pros and cons: to do "the right thing and the clean thing," which is to return Miss Watson's slave, or to do the wicked thing and refuse to harden himself against the man who is his friend. "All right," he decides, "then I'll go to hell."

This is the decision of the natural creature who knows spontaneously what is good and right, no matter what his society's codes. The virtues Huck prizes in his own moral universe are those of candor, loyalty, truth-telling, which would never have come clear to him if it had not been for Jim. They are the virtues mocked and undermined all along the river—in the frauds perpetrated by the Duke and Dauphin, in the killing done by the lordly Colonel Sherburn, who tells the townspeople that "the average man is a coward." (Saying that, he effectively makes each one a "half-man," unable to avenge the murder of the drunken Boggs, "the best naturedest old fool in Arkansaw.")

A circus follows in the same dilapidated town. Throughout the journey down the river there has been a constant shifting of mood like this: horror is transformed into good-natured jawing, or rough and tumble play-acting, which then inevitably gives way to the deadly serious again. Huck, seeing it through his childish eyes, telling it in his plain vernacular, is most directly affected by his involvement in the feud between the Grangerfords and the Shepherdsons. They are "well-born"; their mode of life is gentlemanly, courtly, full of knightly grace. But the two families have been at war with each other over the generations, even though, as young Buck tells Huck, there is no good reason to try to kill the Shepherdsons—"only it's on account of the feud."

Huck, following his instinct, carries a message from a Shepherdson to Sophia Grangerford and innocently contributes to their elopement. This leads to the last stage of the feud, the nighttime ambush in the woods; and Huck, hiding in a tree, sees Buck, his brothers, and their father killed.

> It made me so sick I most fell out of the tree. I ain't a-going to tell *all* that happened—it would make me sick again if I was to do that. I wished I hadn't ever come ashore that night to see such things. I ain't ever going to get shut of them—lots of times I dream about them.

The romantic myth of domestic style and chivalry is exposed. The abstractions of civilization, the causes, what Hemingway was one day to call "words like sacrifice and glory" are rendered meaningless. There remain the ineffectual prescriptions of the heart, which, in the murky world of the new day, lead too often to dead ends.

The awkward ending, with the reversion to Tom's fantasy world and the scheme to free an already liberated Jim, may be a revelation of hopelessness. Returning to the village, Huck has even lost his ability to see Jim as a person. He allows himself to play with him as if he were an object, or a character in an infant's pantomime.

But horror breaks up the children's games. Jim tells Huck that the dead man in the frame house on the river was Huck's own father, and that Jim had covered him so as to protect the boy from seeing. We are left with a complete awareness of Jim's dignified humaneness and maturity. Huck, in contrast, has found the natural code as useless in the village world as was the Sunday school outside. He can only retreat into childishness, however, or fondle dreams of lighting out once more: ". . . she's going to adopt and to sivilize me, and I can't stand it. I been there before."

The school is one of the modes of "sivilizing." The problem of making it relevant to youthful experience and, at the same time, to contemporary demand was becoming more complex than it had ever been. And, as indicated by contemporary literary preoccupations with "lighting out" in search of meanings, the problem is not yet solved today. In Huck Finn's tradition, Ernest Hemingway's Nick Adams goes off beyond the settlements in *In Our Time*; John Steinbeck's inhabitants of Cannery Row are rejecting being "sivilized"; Saul Bellow's *The Adventures of Augie March* deals with a hero who wants to be "adopted," but not by a village Sunday school. Most poignant may be the plight of J. D. Salinger's Holden Caulfield in *The Catcher in the Rye*—the boy whose schools have been as "phony" as the occupations of the city middle class, who tries in vain to wash the dirty words off the walls of his sister's public school, and who wants to be only a "catcher" of children—and protect them from falling into the adult world. Things are meaningless and "sick-making," as Salinger's Franny, in a different educational context, says. So it was in the days after the Civil War, perhaps particularly in the Midwestern places, where farmers were trying to shore up communities like those Huck Finn had seen on the "dangersome" and caving riverbanks.

They were emblematic of the first American settlers, and their villages were shored-up vestiges of the Heavenly Cities which schools had been expected to sustain. Slowly, the farmers became resentful of what was happening to them in the industrially oriented age. Some of them came together to form the National Grange, which began making increasingly militant demands, among which were demands for adequate public schools. The National Educational Association, interpreting this as a sign of "popular upheaval," for the first time began to pay heed to the special needs of rural youth.

In the midst of the Populist agitation of the 1880s and 1890s, farmers spoke about teaching that would be relevant to farming and to rural community life. They won experiment stations here and there, and agricultural institutes. They asked, through their organizations and newspapers, for "useful" knowledge, curricula geared to the understanding of farming, teachers equipped to initiate children into the lives they would actually live.

Irrelevance and abstractness were protested in a desire to win back a sense of self-respect as participants in American life. Without meaningful education, it seemed doubtful if the Huck Finns among them could be kept from striking out for the territories— or worse, the urban frontiers. Surely the schools had the capacity to educate as well as the river did; surely they could become more "scientific" in their handling of vocations than natural experience alone.

But, most of all—in country as in city—something was needed to recreate meaningfulness in the lives of thousands of ordinary people. Lacking it, a most tragic skepticism would take over in those too severely buffeted by change. Mark Twain's *The Mysterious Stranger* held intimations, in the ambiguous comfort offered by Satan's revelation. Nothing exists, neither God, universe, nor human race, he said. "It is all a dream—a grotesque and foolish dream."

11

THE CHILD AND THE
DYNAMO
Schooling in a "Gilded Age"

In the cities the challenge was most concentrated and dramatic; and, when it was confronted squarely, the way was open for sweeping educational change. There were unprecedented numbers in the cities, among them the ones Jacob A. Riis was to describe in *Children of the Poor*: the immigrant youth whose only future lay in the shops and mills, in railroad yards, on docks at the Great Lakes or the sea.

Chicago was becoming the hub of the railway systems and preparing to be "Hog Butcher" and "Tool Maker" for the world. Immigrants were pouring in monthly, filling the construction gangs, manning the machines in Cleveland and Detroit as well. In the 1880s, the first shiploads of eastern and southern European immigrants had begun landing in New York. They were the advance guard of a new sort of pilgrimage: poor, unskilled men and women, oppressed and persecuted at home. Moreover, they were "foreign" in a way previous immigrants had not been. The Irish peasants of the 1840s had spoken a brand of English; the German emigrés of the midcentury had been skilled craftsmen or intellectuals, easily assimilable in many parts of the land.

The Eastern cities were most affected by an infiltration of more than a million people in the peak year, 1902. The "melting pot" was already boiling. New York, particularly, became a city of ghettos, not only Jewish but Italian, Greek, Slavic, Armenian, and, as the twentieth century went on, Southern Negro as well. Once again, great rifts appeared between parents and their children. Language separated them, as the younger generation picked

up English. Traditional authority gave way, as old-country parents lost prestige in the eyes of their children; and, whether the
young conformed to or rejected "the American way," they found
little to identify with in the lives of alien fathers, who were in any
case demeaned by menial jobs in sweatshops or the streets.

The poorly taught, barren elementary schools held little of
value for the children of immigrants. They suffered from a felt
irrelevance, as did the farmers' children; they saw the many
discrepancies between the skills and virtues stressed in school
and those that were rewarded on the streets. The three *R*s, the
McGuffey-style preachments, the drills and punishments—all
these removed the school from what they knew as "reality."
Whether alienated because they were sensitive and "artistic," or
simply because they were estranged from authority figures and
laid open to the ambiguities of the world, many of them resembled the hero of Willa Cather's "Paul's Case," written after the
immigration peak had passed.

Paul finds school "repulsive." He lies when asked whether he
wants to be taken back after being suspended, because he finds
lying "indispensable for overcoming friction." He steals; he runs
away to the Waldorf in New York; he revolts against "the homi-
lies by which the world is run." His revolt is unsuccessful, perhaps
because he is too sensitive to be assuaged—or motivated—by the
images of material success. Other youngsters, similarly attracted
to "glamour" or wealth, were aroused by talk of easy money and
success to such a degree that they were willing to learn any
dodge needed to attain what might be theirs.

Some read or heard about Horatio Alger's carefully wrought
myth as embodied in *Ragged Dick or Mark, the Match Boy*.
Dick, beginning as shoeshine boy, has "a frank, straight-forward
manner," despite his rags and dirty face. He is likable enough to
be favored by Mr. Whitney and others. Because he is honest,
hard-working, and eager to leave behind a "vagabond life," he
can at last plan "to press onward, and rise as high as possible."
Become Richard Hunter, Esq., at last, he proceeds to help an-

other deserving lad, Mark Manton, the match boy. It is mere chance that accounts for Mark's discovery of his wealthy grand-father at the end, but Alger made it clear that he would never have found his "comfortable and even luxurious home" if he had not been so deserving in his match-selling days.

Those immigrants' sons who were influenced by Alger under-standably believed that the disciplines needed for "fame and for-tune" were more likely to be learned in the "school of life" than in the public school. Finding the teaching they received in class-rooms external to their needs, they frequently left school when very young and went to work. Unlike the hero of William Dean Howells' *The Rise of Silas Lapham*, who had grown up on a farm, they did not begin their rise to success with the traditional homely virtues. Unlike Silas Lapham, they were not equipped to confront the elegance of the upper classes with a gentle pride in "stalwart achievement" or an awareness of their own background in the land. They were the alienated persons of the time so far as many groups were concerned. They were aggressively self-reliant, creatures of the city crowds.

The first novelist to render something of the atmosphere sur-rounding them was Stephen Crane. His short novel *Maggie: A Girl of the Streets* was written in 1893 but remained unpublished until he had made his name. His materials were not unlike Al-ger's; but Maggie, in her purity and innocence, lives in an environ-ment molded by necessities so grueling that no small individual could be lucky enough to escape. Rendering Rum Alley, the au-thor was describing what he himself had known. Communicating, as the Impressionist painters were doing, by means of momen-tary sensations, he wrote:

A wind of early autumn raised yellow dust from cobbles and swirled it against a hundred windows . . . garments fluttered from fire-escapes . . . there were buckets, brooms, rags, and bottles. In the street infants played or fought with other in-fants or sat stupidly in the way of vehicles . . . women, with

uncombed hair and disordered dress, gossiped while lean-
ing on railings. . . . The building quivered and creaked from
the weight of humanity stamping about in its bowels.

For the first time, an American was contemplating groups and
neighborhoods in this fashion, feeling "the weight of humanity"
in its pain and poverty—and finding in it the nobility of tragedy.
Maggie, walking out of the bright restaurant district into dark
streets, enters a factory neighborhood where tall buildings loom
over the oily river, and where the water is lit with "a yellow
glare." She drowns herself; her gluttonous and vulgar mother
forgives her when she hears of it, because her life "was a curse
an' her days were black. . . ."

Whether concerned with the defeated street girl or a farm boy
caught in the ebb and flow of a battle he cannot understand,
Crane was trying to image an American Everyman, driven by
multiple forces more powerful than he. They might be the forces
within—the greeds, the twisted passions, pride; they might be
the physical forces of nature, or the drives and intentions of other
men. In his stories, there are strongly felt personalities, intricate
fields of energy, sometimes presented through the consciousness
of the central figure (as through Henry Fleming's in *The Red
Badge of Courage*), sometimes through the mind of a participant
observer (as in "The Blue Hotel" and "The Open Boat").

He presented a rhythmic play of forces: the smoke and "fur-
nace roar" of battle, the dusty faces, rifle flames, the "machinery
of orders," the fear. Or he worked with images of a frozen
prairie, a blizzard, a card game beside a stove in a blue hotel—
and arms of fighters flying in the dark. Or with surf and dark sea,
the beady eyes of a gull, a man waving his coat on a beach—and
four survivors in a lifeboat asking the gods to let them live because they have "worked so hard."

All meshed into fabrics of determinism, or cause and effect relationships. But there was always a shifting spot of light and color
where the human being stood, a being who was in some sense
free. Dwarfed by what surrounded him, perhaps, he nonetheless

was brilliantly defined against the "collaboration" between man and fatality which accidentally awarded badges of courage now and then, or accidentally drowned a sailor within sight and touch of the shore.

Crane's was a vision of entanglement and vulnerability which involved Americans of all sorts, laborers as well as profiteers. There had never been so many overwhelming cities filled with strangers, filled with excessively rich men—and thousands who were desperately poor. Nor had there been so many workingmen aware of being treated as commodities. Suddenly, instead of feeling like frontiersmen or whaling men, Americans were confronting impersonality in economic and social trends which belittled everyone. And their protests were weaker than they had been—and, by the end of the century, resigned. Crane wrote:

> A man said to the Universe:
> "Sir, I exist!"
> "However," replied the universe,
> "The fact has not created in me
> A sense of obligation."

There were implications for education for those who chose to see; but still, in the 1890s, the spokesmen for the school were talking complacently out of allegiance to the *status quo*. While United States Commissioner of Education and afterward, William Torrey Harris represented them when he talked of order and respect for authority and teaching essential "moral duties" to every child.

Certain workingmen took it upon themselves to do battle for their own selfhood and autonomy. It had taken time for them to realize that they could no longer rely upon traditional egalitarian relationships between small businessmen and their employees. Even more slowly than an earlier generation had adapted itself to working in factories, the mass of laboring men had become accustomed to the idea of large industry. One of their early leaders recognized that labor was "a commodity of a peculiar sort," actu-

ally a part of the person who put it up for sale. The grim understanding of this deepened as the years went on; and, early in the
twentieth century, Samuel Gompers, founder of the American
Federation of Labor, was to greet the Clayton Act as labor's
"Magna Carta" because it specifically ruled that labor was *not* a
commodity.

During the first days of widespread labor organization after
the Civil War, the plight of the workingman had been intensified
by a series of Supreme Court decisions dealing with the nature
of a "person" and culminating in interpretations of the Fourteenth Amendment as protecting the "life, liberty, or property"
of corporations viewed as artificial "persons" and, in that guise,
to be protected against the incursions of state laws. The National
Labor Union and others, responding, focused mainly on the eight-
hour day and the necessity to elevate the working class by giving
them enough time for "enlightenment." In this indirect fashion,
men like William H. Sylvis thought, the power of the corporations would eventually be curtailed.

More influential, during the fifteen years of its life, was the
organization known as the Knights of Labor. Originally organized as a secret society, it became an organization similar to an
industrial union soon after the Civil War. Not only were workingmen of all sorts admitted; craftsmen were taken in, clerks, intellectuals, even certain small businessmen. As noteworthy is the
fact that Negroes and women were welcomed equally.

The Knights' stated purposes were more moral and educational than economic or political; but their ultimate aim was to
establish a nationwide cooperative economy. The projected co-
operatives would be owned by the producers themselves, doing
away with wage slavery and the treatment of workingmen as objects rather than as autonomous individuals. Individualism would
be finally harmonized with community. Workingmen, first learning to call each other "Brother," would learn to live in a society of
"brother-men," all equally enlightened, all self-employed.

In their meetings, the Knights tried to do what Pestalozzi and
Robert Owen had said the schools should do: make "men out of

beggars." Knowing the conservatism of the educational leaders, they did not look to the public schools to liberate workingmen. When they argued for the value of "education," they were referring to the informal, uplifting messages of their own speakers and leaders and to the arbitration procedures, the only strictly "union" function they performed.

The very iteration of their demands shed light upon the ambiguous function of the common school in an industrial age. The public school people supported all the efforts taken to weaken the unions; they spoke no language in common with the men meeting in union halls. When the federal government intervened to break the railroad strike of 1877, the educators applauded. Like Horace Mann, they saw the worst sort of mob violence in a strike. They thought it their responsibility to uphold all measures taken in defense of "securities and sanctities." And, in 1886, the public schoolmen, speaking through the National Education Association, again attacked the workers for their part in the notorious Haymarket affair. They said nothing about the occasion for the Haymarket strike or about the official shift of blame to "Anarchists." (It was Haymarket, in fact, that finally destroyed the Knights of Labor, who, for all their hostility to the strike weapon, had been connected with the incidents at the place where the bomb went off.)

The educators' attitude toward the unions did not reflect their attitude toward workers as a class. There were times, indeed, when they seemed to be in open competition with the trade unions for working-class fidelity. The school's prime concern still was to induct the children of laboring men into society at large and, in doing so, to create a social "balance wheel."

In their eagerness to show the workers that the schools could do more for them than could the unions, groups of educators began to interest themselves in specific sorts of training appropriate for working-class children. Not surprisingly, their interest coincided with their desire to serve employers more adequately by providing "better" workers with more developed skills.

When, therefore, the 1876 Philadelphia Centennial Exposition combined with its technological displays exhibits of draw-ings and models done at the Moscow Imperial Technical School, the curiosity of a number of school administrators was aroused. They began asking questions about the graded methods of teach-ing vocational skills developed in the Russian "instruction shops"; and it was in the course of finding answers that they sowed the seeds of the "manual training" movement which soon attracted the attention of businessmen as well as those engaged in voca-tional or "trade school" work.

Those most interested in manual training were hostile to the apprenticeship practices of the unions. They talked of the dig-nity of labor being diminished when skills were taught in factory settings. They charged the unions with arbitrary and "nativist" exclusion policies. There was talk, at the end of the century, of making manual training schools out of many of the common schools.

Professional leaders like William Torrey Harris did not object to manual training *per se*, but they argued against the attenua-tion of "cultural" programs then existing in the schools. The con-troversy over manual training gradually became a debate between exponents of traditionalism and formalism and the defenders of what Harris sardonically called "Rousseauism" or what others called education "according to nature." The debate was fed by the adherents of "nature study" appearing among the rural edu-cators, and the growing enthusiasm for activity-centered class-rooms in various parts of the East and Midwest. Changes were occurring on all sides, compelling groups of all persuasions to pay heed—often for the first time—to the schools.

Most significant was the vast increase in the school population during the final decades of the nineteenth century. Industries had altered too drastically to find women workers and child la-bor as desirable as they had been; and, as the workers' organiza-tions grew, they began to resist the spread of child labor—in self-interest as well as from the humanitarian point of view. The states (usually without positive support from educators) were be-ginning to enact child-labor legislation. What with continually increasing immigration, more and more unemployed children began to appear on the city streets; delinquency became more frequent; and there was a demand for compulsory-attendance legislation in the industrial states. (Massachusetts had passed such legislation before the Civil War.) Once attendance laws were adopted, thousands of children appeared in the schools who would never have been seen there in earlier days. Great numbers of them were dull, uninterested, troublesome; they confronted schoolteachers who were prepared only for selected groups, sent voluntarily by parents with ambitions for their young.

The strain on the schools had been increased when, in 1874, the Kalamazoo Decision sanctioned the public's right to tax-supported high schools; and the new pressures on the schools from below made urgent the necessity for new approaches, new programs—new conceptions of how children might be taught and of the ends toward which mass public schools might strive.

Once again, attention was directed toward the kinds of undertaking associated with the name of Pestalozzi, as well as towards the "scientizing" of instruction being described by the Herbartian Society, in many ways a society of latter-day Pestalozzians. Among those perceptive enough to have anticipated some of the challenges was Edward A. Sheldon, founder of a "ragged" school for poor children in Oswego before the Civil War and later Superintendent of the Oswego public schools. Like many of his contemporaries, he had adapted certain of the more simplistic approaches to Pestalozzi's "object lesson" technique (as satirized, for instance, in the teaching of Mr. Gradgrind in Charles Dickens' *Hard Times*). But he was able, during the Civil War, to establish an influential normal school which helped to revolutionize teaching techniques.

The language used at Oswego often resembled the language of the manual training movement, partly because of the interest in the use of graded methods in the training school. Demonstration teaching was done there; deliberate training in methods was for the first time carried out. There was much talk of the "laws of childhood"; it was sometimes asserted that Oswego was a "philosophic" normal school. In any case, as teacher training began moving in the direction of professional education, it was swept recurrently by Spencerian, Herbartian, or "new educational" breezes. And sometimes there were echoes of demands that the school begin again to find its sanctions in nature, in child development, in the fullness of life itself. The manual training movement was soon rendered archaic by mechanization in industry and the obliteration of traditional trades; but there were residues in talk against the abstract and sterile, against the formal subject-matter areas impermeable to experience in flux.

The more the modern period advanced, the denser became the substance of all that played upon and was touched by the life of the schools. It became increasingly clear that the American school was guided by no overarching design in its development, that no implicit "purpose" had determined the direction of its growth.

Public-spirited men and self-interested men alike had found—and were finding—roles to play. There were those involved who feared men in their collectivities, who thought mainly of restraining them by means of education—keeping saddles on their backs. And there were others who nurtured ideal hopes for ordinary human beings granted life and liberty and equal rights; and still others who saw the American people simply as mankind in its diversity, in its unimaginable depths as well as on the heights. All left marks of some sort on the schools.

There were, as well, individuals who never thought of themselves as being connected with education but who helped shape perspectives on the schools in secret ways. Perhaps it was by forming responses to particular dimensions of cultural life, which may or may not have seemed relevant at first to what was learned and taught. Or perhaps it was by seeing possibilities of human development, or by identifying modes of choosing—or simply by suggesting the ambiguities and complexities of growing and remaining alive.

There had been perplexities and polarities from the beginning, never quite alleviated by the paeans of optimists in the educational world. People had been saying, since the founding of the schools, that education guided by Trade involved a sacrifice of "Man Thinking"—of the one who marched to the sound of his own drum. People had been warning of the temptations in a frontier America, the seductions of opportunity, the dangers of knowing too much and extending one's powers too far.

At the turn of the century, many men were similarly concerned. We have seen Colonel Francis Parker at work in Quincy, Massachusetts. In 1883, he began work at the Cook County Normal School in Chicago, where he discovered that "better homes, better society, better institutions" were required if "civilization," or each American child's destiny, were to be achieved. But it seemed to him that "child study" would provide the magic key, not social remaking. The work of G. Stanley Hall, the psychologist who pioneered the child-study movement, seemed more important to Parker than any existing program for social change.

Hall, in his turn, worked to elucidate the stages of growth as no one had ever done before. His expression of a credo, however, was as generalized and wishful as Parker's: the school, he wrote, would find its guidance in psychology one day; when it did, individuality would at last be given "its full rights as befits a republican government. . . ." He saw "the higher maturity of the superman" being achieved in schools in time to come—images reminiscent of Thoreau surveying the world.

There remained the "herds of men" of which Thoreau had complained, and the "dirty institutions" which weighed them down; and contemporaries of Hall did not share his hopes for science or his stubborn perfectionism. William Dean Howells, editor, novelist, and defender of "realism" against mawkishness and sentimentality in art, had moved, in the 1890s, from the writing of comedies of manners through "commonplace" studies of ordinary life. He was writing protest novels in the spirit of the Socialists of the time. In such books as *A Traveler from Altruria*, he was pointing out the inhumanities of capitalism and the discrepancy which still existed between the American ideal and the reality. What good, he was asking, would education do for children fated to grow up to be laborers? What leisure would they have, what inclination, "to apply the little learning they get in the public schools for . . . personal culture"? How could the superior person of Hall's psychology survive along the railroad yards and factories? Would employers tolerate a "superman"?

Henry Adams, descendant of the family which had done so much to shape America, told the story of his country when he wrote his autobiography at the beginning of the twentieth century. It was, as he saw it, a story of individual failures and the loss of sustaining faiths and certainties. As he saw it, the essential conflict was represented by the contrast between the values symbolized by the medieval Virgin and the values symbolized by the modern "Dynamo." His "education" had not prepared him for the contemporary world, just as American idealism had not prepared Americans to cope with the expansion of industry and the growth of corporations. The Enlightenment beliefs (those of his ancestor, John Adams, as well as those of Thomas Jefferson) had been functions of a Newtonian worldview, now invalidated by the sciences. Men were finding themselves, as Adams put it, driven by forces they had never learned how to name. It was not that he thought Americans should join the Catholic Church (as Orestes Brownson had done half a century before); nor did he believe they could attempt to recreate the eighteenth-century style of life. New orders were required, tragic modes of seeing life, perhaps. The traditional Dream had to be reconceived, if total disillusionment was to be withstood and Americans equipped to deal with change.

In his austere, often esoteric fashion, Adams was expressing the feelings of many observers of the age. He was not alone in recognizing that Americans could no longer depend on something "given"—be it frontier, progress, or Promised Land. There had been intimations of this in imaginative literature for almost seventy years. In education, the effects of what had happened had scarcely been articulated, despite the overwhelming challenge presented to the common school ideal. Here a Harris was trying to subsume all change under a rational world order; there a Parker was trying to keep alive a vision of nature as a dependable source of spontaneity and freedom. In the background Summer's "Social Darwinism" was drumming away: nature, scientifically described, meant impersonal selection processes, that was all; it implied a struggle for survival that sanctioned not the emergence of a "saunterers" or "supermen," but the continuation of a capitalist way of life.

Literature, still pointing metaphorically, giving secret signs of what was happening, shifted its focus from the individual finding fulfillment in the "territory ahead" to human creatures enacting social roles in villages and towns, "determined" (sometimes hopelessly) by environment and heredity. Artists more and more frequently reacted to what they understood of science by painting images of men reduced in stature—"dwarfed" in the way Emerson had predicted. The hero of old, the proud eighteenth-century frontiersman, could but be destroyed, they were saying, if (like an Ahab) he tried to "know" or overcome the powers that determined his life. He could become, perhaps, a hardworking Silas Lapham, if he were fortunate; more likely he would be a Tom Sawyer, playing childish games. From another viewpoint, however, he would be a Henry Fleming, moved back and forth as Stephen Crane's young hero was, aware only of what William James described as "buzzing, booming sensation," blind to purpose and cause. Or he might be someone like Frank Norris' brute McTeague, a product of unalloyed "natural selection," driven by biological drives. Or he might be a "hero" like Theodore Dreiser's Clyde Griffiths in *An American Tragedy*, compelled by an irresistible social environment to destroy himself.

The strategies demanded by education were, inevitably, different from those defined by imaginative literature. Schoolmen could not simply absorb and interpret impinging attitudes and ideas; they could not simply express how the world felt to them. Also, caught up in a meshwork of viewpoints and demands, they were not entitled to do their work in the light of personal visions alone. They were responsible to the community, or to what they were able to conceptualize as the culture. They were asked to present ideas and make decisions in the light of some, if not all, of the manifold interests working in society. They were expected to test their views against the factual information available to them and, at once, against the will of the "grass roots." Literature might embody intimations of what would *become* a predominant challenge to the schools; but the schoolmen's responses necessarily lagged behind the artists'. They had to labor in an entirely public vineyard; the changes they could bring about were conditioned by the seasons of opinion and by the nourishment available in the economic ground.

An instance of this can be seen in the delayed response to the work of the self-taught sociologist Lester Ward, who in 1883 had published a book called *Dynamic Sociology*. Influenced, as Sumner and others had been, by the work of Herbert Spencer and the evolutionists, Ward drew inferences of a unique kind; and, in defining what Darwinian theory "meant," he was able to confront some of the problems confounding the artists of his day—problems still too difficult to be met by schools.

One had to do with the implications of the sciences for man's vision of himself. The other had to do with the hope or progress in the altered world. The objective absence of purpose and design revealed by evolution, Ward had said, increased man's potential freedom instead of negating it. The human being possessed the capacity to take charge of his own further evolution, blind though natural selection had previously been. This was because of the emergence of mind or "mindfulness" in nature, a distinctive mode of adaptation which permitted human beings to direct evolution in their social worlds. It followed, as Ward conceived it, that education was the most important means of insuring a socially desirable (and humanly desirable) movement forward. Public, preferably universal, education would enable each society to assimilate in time and to transmit the range of "individual achievement which has civilized the world."

When Ward's work was at last publicized in the 1890s, there were educational thinkers at work who were ready to seize upon such insights and incorporate them into theories of teaching to the end of improving the quality of social life. The relation between the natural and the social had been altered once more in Ward's design. It was at least possible to imagine continuing progress, progress that would now be man's to make, social man's, alone.

Then, in 1891, Herman Melville died, after living for thirty years in virtual retirement from literature. He left a short novel, *Billy Budd Foretopman*, which was not to be printed until 1924, a novel that enacted in its own way what Ward had discovered, and what John Dewey and his co-workers would attempt to incorporate in approaches to the public schools.

The scene of Melville's story is a warship, the *Indomitable*, a harbinger, perhaps, of regulated societies to come. When Billy Budd unintentionally kills Mr. Claggert, he is tried by a drumhead court of ship's officers who are inclined to be merciful to "Baby Budd." He had meant no harm and Claggert, the master-at-arms, had represented the worst in "natural depravity." Their inclination is to act as naturally as Huck Finn did when he chose to "go to hell." But Captain Vere reminds them that it is wartime and that England is threatened by mutinies. The Mutiny Act governs them, he says—not Nature, but "the King," identified with society.

> Though the ocean, which is inviolate Nature primeval, tho' this be the element where we move and have our being as sailors, yet as the King's officers lies our duty in a sphere correspondingly natural?

Once they received their commissions, he tells the officers of the court, they "in the most important regards, ceased to be natural free-agents."

In a sense, Captain Vere's may be heard as the voice of the century's finale, and the voice that announces what is about to be. Men were beginning to learn that there could be neither "lighting out" nor retreat in America any longer. They were beginning to learn that their only hopes were to be found in human modes of ordering, in human "mindfulness." For a moment, when the new century opened, there was a burst of hope, as if mutinies could never occur again, as if Mutiny Acts might give way to designs for living deliberately. And it seemed, it may be for the last time, that education might at length remake the unhappy world, that individual fulfillment might finally flower in community—that the common school might keep the promise and bring redemption to all.

12

". . . TOMORROW WE WILL RUN FASTER. . . ."

Melville's ocean had been an emblem of dark Necessity, with disorder in the depths. Writers and educators both began thinking more and more about the need for barriers—against senselessness, violence, social unrest. But activist forces began gathering in the last decade of the nineteenth century. Farmers organized the short-lived Populist movement. Labor unions, outraged by the breaking of the Homestead and Pullman strikes, began to stir with talk of class hate. The panic of 1893 and the lean years after resulted in unemployment, reduced wages, poverty. Industrial consolidation led to the appearance of giant trusts and cartels; the few millionaires surviving became exemplars of inequality. The resulting polarization began to alarm the middle and professional classes. The dream of equality was being too blatantly betrayed; the dignity of those who spoke for America seemed on the verge of being destroyed.

Abruptly, then, in the transformed world of city people and factories, reform began: with the beginning of the twentieth century, Progressivism took hold. In many respects, it was like a re-creation of the Enlightenment; men dreamed of upward progress once again and expected a Promised Land. They knew, however, that it could only be deliberately constructed by human beings now, by educated people, in a world that was rational and just. The humanitarians and reformers and "muckrakers" began exposing and proposing hopefully. Sociological and psychological knowledge was to be put to work in social life. There were to be reawakening and reconstruction in the light of an intelligent, a moral, ideal.

The antagonists were defined as the financiers and industrialists, who exploited working men by the thousand and manipulated local governments as well. They were full-blooded, excessive personalities, living reminders of the Gilded Age. Even the Carnegies among them, the virtuous Presbyterians who called themselves "custodians" of wealth, began to anger those who looked upon them and arouse the slumbering Puritan conscience of the "middle class."

Contemplatives and saints would be ineffectual in fighting them; vigorous men were needed, as excessive in their own way as the corporation pioneers. Appropriately, Theodore Roosevelt, the Progressivists' President, was an exponent of the "strenuous life" and at once a respecter of empirical minds. The journalists, the "muckrakers" who helped to educate the public, were themselves aggressive characters, making full use of the newly available popular press in its cheapness and sensationalism.

Lincoln Steffens, the best-known of the crusading journalists, could render reality as accurately as a naturalistic novelist. He exposed corruption and injustice in their ugliness and their colorful variety; and, while doing so, he managed to communicate a moral view of life centering on responsibility. He believed that the "system" was more to blame than its representatives. He was more concerned about the consequences of behavior for the welfare and moral condition of the people in general than he was about the virtue or villainy of particular politicians or businessmen. Like many Progressives, Steffens was convinced that the public could be and should be educated into taking responsibility. Through verbal exhortation, somehow, the urban sense of anonymity could be overcome, he thought. Despite the crowds, the tenements, the factories changing the face of America, the conviction of personal efficacy could finally be restored.

Laws were being passed at the same time, some of them a response to what the journalists exposed. Monopolies were controlled, as were the excesses of the trusts. Child welfare was protected in several areas; labor unions were assured a range of freedoms; the way was prepared for direct political action through initiative and referendum; income taxes began to narrow the distance between the extremes of wealth and poverty. Some legislation was on a state level, much on a federal level; and the movement lasted through the early days of Woodrow Wilson's administration, until the first world war.

The Supreme Court, becoming "functionalist" and empirical in its orientation, handed down decisions written in the light of anticipated consequences for society. Like the justices, members of the legal profession across the country were responding to new approaches to society, new perceptions of the nature of man. The discoveries being made in the social sciences were as inescapable as those in physics and biology. It began to seem illicit for intelligent men to govern themselves not by "science," but by prejudice or by precedent alone.

Wherever there was intellectual inquiry, there was an intense methodological concern. Fruitfulness was used as the criterion when men were asked to judge *how* things ought to be done, what decisions ought to be made. Franz Boas was developing empirical techniques in anthropology, Thorstein Veblen in economics, the Beards in the study of history. And they were but the leaders in a movement almost coextensive with the academic world. Scholars were beginning to study processes of social life and thought, applying intelligence to the pursuit of progressive ends. There were many who were attempting interdisciplinary studies with similar objectives in mind: Vernon L. Parrington, the literary historian; philosophers like Charles Sanders Peirce, William James, Josiah Royce.

Launching his work in the 1870s, Peirce was quietly providing the philosophic armature for much of what was to happen in the thinking of the 1900s. Originating, perhaps, in the preoccupation with blind chance and disorder that troubled so many contemporaries, Peirce's thinking produced a design for moving from chance to meaningful order. Thought and action, as he described them, could be joined by "scientific intelligence," if properly used. Human beings, understanding ideas in terms of their *effects*, could be taught how to overcome the discrepancies, the splits in their experience. The object was to build "good habits" of thinking—to attain a dependable state of rationality.

William James, for a time Peirce's Harvard colleague, explained that the rationality desired was not intended to resemble the certainty of the "mousetrap," which was what he called all closed systems of philosophy, like the dominant Hegelianism of the day. Then, choosing to diverge from Peirce's view, James said that even rationality was not the most desirable end there was. It was good to become as reasonable as possible because reason had the capacity of showing the range of options confronting individuals—the possibilities of willing and acting, choosing and becoming personally free. Meaning, truth itself, James said, ought to be judged not merely by their contributions to rational understanding. The most important test was the degree to which they enriched individual experience in the open world, the degree to which they made satisfactions possible.

Peirce and James were philosophic pragmatists, both concerned with the fruitfulness and the consequences of intelligent thought. But James moved closer to the Enlightenment ideal than the commitment to rationality itself actually required. He was interested in the release of individuality above all things, in the maintenance of a realm of indeterminacy, of openness for the human spirit in the midst of a casually determined world. There were echoes of Emerson in what he wrote, echoes of his Transcendentalist father, Henry James Senior, as well; but they were absorbed in what he called "radical empiricism," his account of the stream of consciousness flowing in the midst of life, acting on the world by means of mind, creating occasions for knowing and fulfilling desire. The idealist Josiah Royce most clearly evoked Emerson when he spoke of communion and community, sometimes in concert with William James, or when he spoke of reality and "personhood" rising out of communication and the meeting of minds.

Ideas like these, working in and below experiment and reform, helped fertilize the ground for innovative thinking about the public school. Traditionally enmeshed in a web of interests and ideals, the school could not but be affected by the progressive atmosphere. That it was not wholly transformed was due to the natural inertia of a cultural agency dependent on individuals for its day-to-day functioning, on neighborhoods for much of its support. Schools could not be dramatically transformed by edict or prescription from above. The Progressive era was too brief for the remaking the schools would have had to undergo to become "Progressive" schools; and, once World War I began, it became questionable whether Progressivism in its original sense would ever be relevant again.

The exemplar of educational Progressivism was John Dewey, whose background so bound the centuries together that his thought sheds particular light on the meaning and limitations of Progressivism—and, perhaps, on the tragedy of the common school. His life story recapitulates many crucial transitions in America; but, unlike an artist like Mark Twain, the transitions were not impasses in his eyes, but (as they were to William James) novel opportunities. He found no refuges in illusions; nor did he hope for escape.

He had been born in Vermont, in small-town America, traditional in character from grist mill to meeting hall. When he attended Johns Hopkins University's graduate school, he fell under the influence of the Hegelian philosophy; his essays before he entered the field of education explored the dialectic, just as Harris' had done. He taught in Michigan, then went to Chicago, arriving in 1894, when the contrast between small-town and city life was most intense. He chaired a large department at the University of Chicago and, while there, experienced the streets of the city, the diverse crowds of immigrants, the slums.

He met Jane Addams, the humanitarian settlement-house worker whose Hull House attracted children from the streets, and artists and scholars as well. Soon afterward, he was at work experimenting in the University Elementary School and in the Laboratory School organized where Parker's demonstration school had been. Later, there was Teachers College at Columbia University, on the edge of the slums in the largest city of all.

Throughout, Dewey experienced continual encounters with the most potent ideas of the time: William James' *Principles of Psychology*; the reports of the Herbartian Society and statements by the kindergarten teachers; the insights of the novel social sciences; selections from the writings of Lester Ward, deepening Dewey's understanding of what may have been most crucial for him—Darwinian biology.

As philosopher and psychologist, Dewey was peculiarly well equipped to integrate the several disciplines relevant to the school. He was prepared to philosophize with respect to education, to interpret proposals pragmatically, to make his own experiential tests of what psychology and sociology entailed for public schools. Because, as he well knew, the life of learning is continuous, he was for a long time equipped with Hegelian categories, even after he entered the educational domain. This helped to determine what he saw, what he attempted to achieve. And because he was in so many ways a mediator of the past, his way of looking at the school has tended to survive—and with it the Hegelian ordering, the Hegelian need to resolve.

His importance here lies more in the imaging and the conceptualizing than in the influence he exerted on the schools of his time. It made a difference to later hopes and expectations that Dewey saw the world around him as a series of overlapping dualities. Not only did contemporary minds, as he perceived them, bifurcate human beings into bodies and minds, and the universe into the natural and supernatural. Not only were the individual and the group dichotomized; theory and practice, work and play. The school, he thought, was viewed in separation from society, the child from the curriculum, education from life itself. The consequence seemed to him to be that the primary objective of inquiry had to be the creation of resolutions, the release of tensions, the reconciliation of the conflicts that blocked and obscured practice in the public schools.

Dewey did not attend, as Peirce was doing, to the physical sci-

ences as much as he did to the biological, especially of the post-
Darwinian years. His mood was predominantly empirical; he was
persistently oriented to verifiable experience. The crucial justification for rationality, for intelligence, he thought, was to be found
in its contribution to the quality of human experience, social experience particularly, in the open world. And the quality of such
experience, the meanings achieved through inquiry, were to be
the central preoccupation of the public school.

Children were to be guided into membership in the society as
they reached out to explore the world by means of the curriculum, as they sought answers to questions framed in situations of
increasing complexity. Growing, forever in search of richer meanings, they would be fulfilling themselves as individuals. Continuing to seek, to find out, they would become participant members
of the adult community. Such a community, made up of distinctive, self-realizing yet cooperative individuals, would in time be
fulfilled as democracy—itself going on to create, to realize an
ever-richer quality of social life.

With such a concept, Dewey incorporated the multiple strains
of Progressive thought. Extending and transcending the Hegelian striving toward a oneness, a harmony, he put empirical method
to work in defining a democratic educational ideal. It becomes
increasingly clear, as the years go on, that both his means and
ends were functions of a particular historic period. On the one
hand, they were derived from the painful discrepancies of the
preceding century, from the need for total resolution, at least
where the school was concerned. On the other hand, they were
reflections of the sense of possibility pervading the Progressive
age. Confidence in intelligence was so extreme that men really
believed in a future that would be democratic, wholly civilized—
a fulfillment, at last, of the Dream. And the common school? The
original promise would at last be kept. The school would release
children to be self-reliant citizens; individualism would give way
to the integrative strivings of diverse individuality. De Tocqueville's fears would be laid to rest. Mann's and Emerson's hopes
would jointly become real.

The United States is still living through the decline of Progressivism and the cutting short by World War I of the Democratic Renascence. Just as the nineteenth-century revolutions undermined the Enlightenment faith in Reason, so did "the war to make the world safe for democracy" shake the belief that intelligence could create a lasting, humane order to serve all of mankind.

Public school spokesmen talked more complacently than ever, once the war was done. They became concerned with meeting the needs of the vast, assorted student body moving into the high schools; abruptly, they had to accommodate "all American youth." Attention oscillated between life-adjustment and job training, as testing and measurement began to suggest more efficient techniques of talent selection for a time of prosperity. Among progressive educators, most of the talk dealt with child study, free expression, or the implications of the new psychologies for what the Transcendentalists had called the realization of the self. Although few expressed diminishing confidence, there was a decline in discussion of abstract "purposes" and of the connection between the goals of schooling and what had so long been the Dream.

There were sporadic efforts to focus social studies on the interlocking forces now seen to be operating in the world; but it was left to literature, once again, to present intimations of what these meant for living men.

Theodore Dreiser, in the very center of Progressive optimism, had begun a portrayal of how things would be in a world shadowed by determinisms. His novels told of passionate, striving human creatures who come into conflict with a pitiless and mercenary society which overwhelms by sheer power. Edwin Arlington Robinson, in 1905, was already writing poems about desperate human beings overcome by financial loss, neglect, and loneliness: "Miniver Cheevy, born too late . . ."; Bewick Finzer, who loses his money, dreams his "dreams of affluence," and keeps returning for a loan. "Familiar as an old mistake,/And futile as regret." In "Cassandra," written in 1916, he told of the doom of those who worship the trinity of "Dollar, Dove, and Eagle," a doom pronounced by a voice that asks, "Are you to pay for what you have/ With all you are?"

>   . . . ——No other word
> We caught, but with a laughing crowd
> Moved on. None heeded, and few heard.

Many artists heard, if not the schoolmen. Sinclair Lewis, bitterly caricaturing the Main Streets of the country, painted the middle-class hero as Babbitt, the man of tawdry ambitions and trivial mind, making a stereotype of the long-lasting Dream. The sensitive, the intellectual—the sharply "individual"—are forever outsiders in the new, respectable American small town. Or they are "grotesques," as in Sherwood Anderson's *Winesburg, Ohio*, each one reaching out to love, to be a brother-man—and being forced (by the adjusted man's passion for size and "mechanical things") back upon himself. Once forced back by the impotence of another, the outsider could not light out, could not go free. He became a cripple, a creature destroyed by repression—no longer a lover but a "grotesque."

There were writers who publicly announced that they had been betrayed. Like Randolph Bourne, many saw themselves deprived of illusion by the Progressive older generation, which had promised so much and delivered hypocrisy, sterility, war. John Dewey and Woodrow Wilson were attacked by Bourne for supporting the war and sacrificing the individual to the national "cause." Bourne saw their early optimism effectually exposed by this "betrayal" of the rational way. The only cause worth fighting for was the cause of the single self, the freedom Thoreau had written of, and Whitman, and Mark Twain.

Many agreed. Some took off to other countries—although, as Ernest Hemingway wrote in *The Sun Also Rises*, "'. . . going to another country doesn't make any difference. I've tried all that. You can't get away from yourself by moving from one place to another. There's nothing to that.'"

162   THE PUBLIC SCHOOL AND THE PRIVATE VISION

For him and a few others, there was the freedom required for learning the discipline of a craft. Resisting fallibility and "whiteness," they struggled to master the experience which traditional terms could not express. When, like Hemingway, they succeeded for a time, they imposed their own authentic form upon the inchoateness of the modern world. A T.S. Eliot, of course, would form it as a wasteland demanding regeneration in a return to faith—or in, as Melville had thought, engagement in the book of the ages, the tragedy of the human past. More frequently, the effort was made to give experience a shape as plain, spare, and transparent as that achieved by the nostalgic Mark Twain.

Today, the men most concerned with education are dealing with curriculum and concept development as the artists of the 1920s were dealing with the stuff of which they made their art. It is as if now, after the concentration camps, Hiroshima, Sputnik, and the rest, after the cumulative attacks on the school, educators have experienced a confrontation. No longer do they address themselves, as in the 1930s, to building "a new social order." Nor do they talk, as in the 1830s, of moralism and defense of the *status quo*. The objective, even where the "slow" and underprivileged are concerned, seems to be to consider education as discipline, as craft—no longer as a carrier of dreams. The new morality of teaching is a morality linked to belief in "making sense," in the usefulness of conceptualization, forming the confusing world. No longer do teachers expect to pierce the "veil": they are preoccupied with instructing in the categories out of which the "real" is now composed. They are logical categories, each one organizing and containing a multiplicity of facts. To know has come to mean to be familiar with cognitive forms. To be has come to be identified with inwardness, at least for some—the existential innerness which escapes all formulas and sermons and cannot be realized by any public Dream.

And what of the Dream, in the glow of which the common school was made? What of the Dream, whose improbability moved men to create a literature of the dark? We may turn one last time to a work of literature for a clue, to a novel dramatizing the Dream. F. Scott Fitzgerald's *The Great Gatsby* does so, as it presents the career of James Gatz, whose "parents were shiftless and unsuccessful farm people—his imagination had never really accepted them as his parents at all."

> The truth was that Jay Gatsby of West Egg, Long Island, sprang from his Platonic conception of himself. He was a son of God—a phrase, which if it means anything, means just that—and he must be about His Father's business, the service of a vast, vulgar, and meretricious beauty.

Gatsby is a twentieth-century exemplar of the pilgrimage and the sense of quest out of which the idea of our schools derived. The son of "shiftless and unsuccessful farm people" (as our schools were descended from the town and charity schools of the past), Gatsby has achieved success by becoming a bootlegger—a latter-day embodiment of the Alger ideal. His manifest goal is the wealthy Daisy Buchanan and the green light across the Bay; but he, too, has been seeking a Whale, a Promised Land, a Heavenly City, without knowing if he is in time, or if the light and shore exist.

Settling in West Egg, Long Island, however, Gatsby still has faith "in the green light, the orgiastic future that year by year recedes. . . ." Daisy, like the traditional hope, may be no more than a memory; she may be gossamer and wishful, without relevance to present need. No matter. It "eluded us then, but . . . tomorrow we will run faster, stretch out our arms farther . . . and one fine morning——"

This has been a book about illusions, about green lights and transcendent goals. Much still depends on whether the goals are attainable, and whether attainment will make a difference to personal life. In Fitzgerald's novel, Nick Carraway, the narrator, discloses some of what may be involved. He forms what happens by observing through a pattern of Midwest, small-town values, like the values of America's past. He was raised in the West, with the moral advantages associated with simpler times. And these enable him to act as witness to what occurs in the pitiless urbanized East—to escape, when all is done, to tell, to give it tragic form.

The events are patterned, therefore, as Nick sees Gatsby in relation to the careless Daisy and her husband, to the Wilsons in the nearby garage. He perceives the decency of Gatsby by means of his own conception of the honorable; he looks through the glamour and the vulgarity into Gatsby's rare fidelity. And he knows that Gatsby has become a kind of hero through his seeking, that he possesses dignity far more than do the Buchanans, who "smashed up things and creatures and then retreated back into their money or their vast carelessness. . . ."

The doubleness of the green beacon now comes clear. Nick places what he sees against the Valley of Ashes, where the eyes of Doctor Eckleburg brood from a billboard over a "solemn dumping ground." Because we can watch the enactments taking place in the focus of a magnified, bespectacled, faceless gaze as well as through Nick Carraway's eyes, we can discover how wrong Gatsby is in thinking the past can be repeated and the Dream held inviolable through time. We can detect for ourselves the "foul dust" in the Eastern air and understand that the loftiest dream—even a dream of enlightenment—is susceptible of contamination, that ideals are always invisibly eroded by the fallibility of men.

The common schools must leave the Gatsbyan innocence behind. The Dream may be maintained if we can define wider and more inclusive meanings, less overweening goals. And we may learn to form, through the traditional vision of a decent dignity, an honorable, comradely pursuit—and to complement the view of the human witness with what is revealed by Doctor Eckleburg's stare.

Bibliography

General Works in the History of American Literature, Education, and Society

Beard, Charles A. and Mary R. *The American Spirit*. New York: Macmillan, 1942, Chapters 5–8. A discussion of the "idea of civilization" as it worked in American life from 1830 to 1900.

Brooks, Van Wyck. *Makers and Finders: A History of the Writer in America*. New York: Dutton, 1936–1952. The last four volumes of this five-volume work provide a complete evocation of American writers and their settings from 1830 to 1915.

Butts, R. Freeman and Lawrence A. Cremin. *A History of Education in American Culture*. New York: Holt, 1953, Chapters 7 and 8, Parts 3 and 4. Far-ranging survey of all aspects of the schools.

Cargill, Oscar. *Intellectual America: Ideas on the March*. New York: Macmillan, 1941. European influences on twentieth-century ideas.

Cunliffe, Marcus. *The Literature of the United States*. London: Pelican Books, 1954. One of the best short histories.

Curti, Merle. *The Growth of American Thought* (3rd ed.). New York: Harper and Row, 1964. An inclusive discussion of American ideas in their social contexts.

————. *The Social Ideas of American Educators*. New York: Scribner, 1935. Chapters 3–15. The pioneering American Historical Association Report on the commitments of educators from Mann to Dewey.

Degler, Carl N. *Out of Our Past: The Forces That Shaped Modern America*. New York: Harper and Row, 1959, Chapters 5–13. A readable and analytic social and political history.

Edwards, Newton and Herman G. Richey. *The School in the American Social Order: The Dynamics of American Education*. Boston: Houghton Mifflin, 1947, Chapters 9–20. A study of the developing school against the socioeconomic background of the changing United States.

Elsbree, Willard S. *The American Teacher*. New York: American Book, 1939. A survey of the shifting roles and changing status of the teacher in America.

Gabriel, Ralph H. *The Course of American Democratic Thought: An Intellectual History Since 1815* (2nd ed.). New York: Ronald, 1956. Particularly perceptive in the areas of Transcendentalism and Progressivism.

Hofstadter, Richard. *Anti-Intellectualism in American Life*. New York: Knopf, 1963. An exhaustive study of a significant theme. Part 5, "Education in a Democracy," is particularly illuminating.

———. *The American Political Tradition*. New York: Vintage. Specific men and ideas, brilliantly presented.

Howard, Leon. *Literature and the American Tradition*. Garden City, N.Y.: Doubleday, 1960, Parts 2 and 3. Studies of empiricism, idealism, and rationalism in literature from Cooper to James.

Larkin, Oliver W. *Art and Life in America*. New York: Holt, 1960. A good introduction to the graphic arts and design.

Matthiessen, Francis O. *The American Renaissance*. New York: Oxford, 1941. Still the classic study of American literary romanticism.

Miller, William, *A New History of the United States*. New York: Braziller, 1958. Good narrative "contextual" history.

Parkes, Henry Bamford. *The American Experience*. New York: Vintage. An interpretative essay on American civilization.

Parrington, V. L. *Main Currents in American Thought*. New York: Harcourt, 1930, Books II and III. The great innovative social history of American letters, written from the Jeffersonian point of view.

Persons, Stow. *American Minds: A History of Ideas*. New York: Holt, 1958, Parts 3–5. A study of the major movements of thought.

Rourke, Constance. *American Humor*. Garden City, N.Y.: Anchor Books. Revelations of American character through folklore and humor.

Schneider, Herbert W. *A History of American Philosophy*. New York: Columbia, 1946, Chapters 5–8. Still the standard overview of philosophic ideas in America.

Spiller, Robert E., Willard Thorp, Thomas H. Johnson, Henry Seidel Canby, *Literary History of the United States* (Rev. one-vol. ed.). New York: Macmillan, 1955.

Welter, Rush. *Popular Education and Democratic Thought in America*. New York: Columbia, 1962. A suggestive effort to relate educational thinking to the several strands of democratic thought.

Wolfe, Don M. *The Image of Man in America*. New York: McGraw-Hill Paperback. A selective intellectual history ranging from Horace Mann to Alfred Kinsey.

1. The Search Begins: Education, Literature, and the Dream

Among useful studies of "the American Dream" as it affected American experiences is E. M. Burns, *The American Idea of Mission* (Rutgers University Press, 1957). A. N. Kaul's *The American Vision* (Yale University Press, 1964) studies the tension between the actual and the ideal as expressed in nineteenth-century American fiction. For relevant critique, see Reinhold Niebuhr's *The Irony of American History* (Scribner, 1952) and Daniel Boorstin's *The Image—or What Happened to the American Dream* (Atheneum, 1962).

Also see Alexis de Tocqueville, *Democracy in America*, Vols. I and II, edited by Phillips Bradley (Vintage). Most relevant are Chapters 14–18 (Vol. I) and Chapters 8–18 (Bk. One, Vol. II); Chapters 1–5, 16–20 (Bk. Two, Vol. II). Themes are struck here which will resound repeatedly.

2. Enlightenment Ideals and "Common Men": From Jefferson to Mann

The definitive study of Thomas Jefferson's concern with education is Roy J. Honeywell's *The Educational Work of Thomas Jefferson* (Harvard University Press, 1931). See Gordon C. Lee (ed.), *Crusade Against Ignorance: Jefferson on Education* (No. 6, Teachers College Classics, 1961) for a wide selection of extracts from Jefferson's papers. James B. Conant's *Thomas Jefferson and the Development of American Public Education* (University of California Press, 1962) is a well-documented evaluation in the light of contemporary developments. Merrill D. Peterson's *The Jefferson Image in the American Mind* (Oxford University Press, 1962) is a suggestive account of changing approaches to Jeffersonianism in the nineteenth and twentieth centuries.

For representative documents from the Jacksonian period, see Edwin C. Rozwenc (ed.), *Ideology and Power in the Age of Jackson* (Anchor). For a fresh view of Jacksonian democracy, see Marvin Meyers, *The Jacksonian Persuasion: Politics and Belief* (Vintage).

Lawrence A. Cremin (ed.), *The Republic and the School: Horace Mann on the Education of Free Men* (No. 1, Teachers College Classics, 1957) presents selections from Mann's annual reports and an essay on his "legacy." For a biography of Mann, see E. I. F. Williams, *Horace Mann: Educational Statesman* (Macmillan, 1937).

3. Transcendentalists, Utopians, and Reformers: The Challenge to "Establishment" and School

For selections from Transcendentalist writings, see Perry Miller (ed.), *The American Transcendentalists: Their Prose and Poetry* (Anchor). There are numerous paperback anthologies of Emerson's chief works, including Eduard C. Lindeman (ed.), *Emerson: The Basic Writings of America's Sage* (Mentor); Alfred Kazin and Daniel Aaron (eds.), *Emerson: A Modern Anthology* (Dell); and Mark Van Doren (ed.), *The Portable Emerson* (Viking).

Van Wyck Brooks' *The Flowering of New England* (Everyman) remains a fine introduction to the literary climate of the period. See Alice Felt Tyler's *Freedom's Ferment* (Harper Torchbook) and Daniel Aaron's *America in Crisis* (Knopf, 1952) for accounts of reformers and utopians of many kinds.

4. The "Balance Wheel" and the Public School Campaigns

On the lyceum movement and the public campaigns for common schools, see Carl Bode, *The American Lyceum: Town Meeting of the Mind* (Oxford University Press, 1956). Consult, too, Henry Barnard's *The American Journal of Education* (1855–1882). For the range of opinions among educators, see Merle Curti's *The Social Ideas of American Educators* (Littlefield, Adams, 1961).

For a detailed account of the McGuffey readers, see Harvey C. Minnich, *William H. McGuffey and His Readers* (University of Cincinnati, 1936). See also *McGuffey's Fifth Eclectic Reader*, with a Foreword by Henry S. Commager (Signet).

5. Nathaniel Hawthorne's "Peep-Hole" View

Hawthorne's novels and short stories are available in a number of paperback editions. See particularly Malcolm Cowley (ed.), *The Portable Hawthorne* (Viking), which includes *The Scarlet Letter*, the major short stories, journals, letters, and a fine Editor's Introduction. See Newton Arvin (ed.), *Hawthorne's Short Stories* (Vintage) and Dolphin editions of *The House of the Seven Gables*, *The Blithedale Romance*, and *The Marble Faun*.

Mark Van Doren's *Nathaniel Hawthorne* (Viking, 1957) is a useful, brief "critical biography." For criticism, see the relevant chapters in Harry Levin, *The Power of Blackness* (Vintage) and in Richard Chase, *The American Novel and Its Tradition* (Anchor).

6. The Classroom at Walden Pond

Thoreau's *Walden* is available in a great many paperback editions, including the Bantam edition (edited by Joseph Wood Krutch), and the Signet edition (edited by Perry Miller). *The Variorum Walden*, annotated and with an introduction by Walter Harding, Secretary of the Thoreau Society (Washington Square Press), is the first paperback based on Thoreau's own copy.

Also in paper are Thoreau's "On the Duty of Civil Disobedience," printed with *Walden* in the Collier Books edition, the Signet edition, and others; *A Week on the Concord and Merrimack Rivers* (Signet); and *A Writer's Journal*, edited by Laurence Stapleton (Dover).

For biographical material on Thoreau, see Henry Seidel Canby, *Thoreau* (Houghton Mifflin, 1939) and Walter Harding, *A Thoreau Handbook* (New York University Press, 1959). Helpful criticism appears in Carl Bode (ed.), *The Young Rebel in American Literature* (Praeger, 1959) and, particularly, in R. W. B. Lewis, *The American Adam* (Phoenix, 1955).

7. Masses, Melting Pots, and Monitors: "Rote" Teaching and Lancastrian Schools

Marvin Meyers, *The Jacksonian Persuasion*, Chapter 11, is an account of the political tumult in New York. For telling vignettes of conditions under which immigrants lived, see Cecil Woodham-Smith, *The Great Hunger* (Signet), pp. 249–66. Also see Morton and Lucia White, *The Intellectual versus the City* (Mentor), dealing with American artists' and thinkers' viewpoints on American cities, including New York.

Further details about the struggle over secularization in New York are in Samuel W. Brown, *The Secularization of American Education* (Teachers College, 1912) and selected issues of *The American Journal of Education*. For accounts of the Lancastrian system, see John Gill, *Systems of Education* (Heath, 1887), John Pancoast Gordy, *Rise and Growth of the Normal School Idea in the United States* (Washington: Government Printing Office, 1891), and Charles D. Brauner, *American Educational Theory* (Prentice-Hall, 1964).

8. ". . . High Time to Go to Sea. . . .": Melville's Vision of America

There are numerous paperback editions of Melville's work, particularly of *Moby-Dick*. See, among others: the Dolphin edition of *Moby-*

Dick; the Bobbs-Merrill edition, edited by Charles N. Feidelson, Jr.; the Modern Library College edition, edited by Leon Howard; the Riverside edition, edited by Alfred Kazin. Also, there are the following editions of Melville's other writings: *Typee* and *Billy Budd* (Everyman), edited by Milton R. Stern; *The Shorter Novels of Herman Melville* (Universal Library); *Herman Melville: Four Short Novels*, including "Bartleby" and "Benito Cereno" (Bantam); *The Confidence-Man* (Evergreen).

Newton Arvin's *Herman Melville* (Viking) is a good critical biography. The most exhaustive and enlightening critique is to be found in Howard P. Vincent, *The Trying-Out of Moby-Dick* (Houghton Mifflin, 1949). Helpful chapters are to be found in Richard Chase, *The American Novel and its Tradition* and Harry Levin, *The Power of Blackness*.

9. The Songs of Selfhood: *En Masse* and the Ideal

Among paperback editions of Whitman's *Leaves of Grass* are Gay Wilson Allen and Charles T. Davis (eds.), *Walt Whitman's Poems* (Evergreen); Mark Van Doren (ed.), *The Portable Walt Whitman* (Viking); the Dolphin edition of *Leaves of Grass* (1855 ed.), and the Cornell University Press edition of *Leaves of Grass* (1860 ed.). See also John Kouwenhoven (ed.), *Leaves of Grass and Selected Prose* (Modern Library College edition); James E. Miller, Jr. ed. *Complete Poetry and Selected Prose* (Rinehart); and the Library of Liberal Arts edition of *Democratic Vistas*.

The definitive biography of Walt Whitman is Gay Wilson Allen's *The Solitary Singer: A Critical Biography of Walt Whitman* (Evergreen). See F. O. Matthiessen's essay on Whitman in his *American Renaissance*, listed in this bibliography under General Works. For evidence of Whitman's interest in Hegel, see W. B. Fulghum, Jr., "Whitman's Debt to Joseph Gostwick" *American Literature*, Vol. XII (1940–1941), pp. 491–96. D. H. Lawrence gives a satirical view of this, in his *Studies in Classic American Literature* (Anchor).

For information about the St. Louis Hegelians, see Charles M. Perry, *The St. Louis Movement in Philosophy: Some Source Material* (University of Oklahoma Press, 1930). Also, see the files of the *Journal of Speculative Philosophy*.

10. The Predicaments of Freedom: The Negro, the Farmer, and Huck Finn

For the "Gilded Age" after the Civil War, see Vernon L. Parrington, *Main Currents in American Thought*, Vol. II (Harvest); Thomas C.

Cochran and William Miller, *The Age of Enterprise: A Social History of Industrial America* (Macmillan, 1942).

For information on Reconstruction and the plight of the Negro in the South, see Paul Buck, *The Road to Reunion, 1865–1900* (Little, Brown, 1937); W. E. B. Du Bois, *Black Reconstruction: An Essay Towards the Part Which Black Folk Played in the Attempt to Reconstruct Democracy in America, 1860–1880* (Harcourt Brace, 1935); C. Vann Woodward, *Origins of the New South, 1870–1913* (Louisiana State University Press, 1951) and *The Strange Career of Jim Crow* (Galaxy). For Booker T. Washington's approach, see *Up From Slavery: An Autobiography* (Doubleday, 1947). Edmund Wilson, "The Ordeal of George W. Cable," *The New Yorker*, November 9, 1957 is an informative essay on George W. Cable. See also George W. Cable, *The Negro Question*, edited by Arlin Turner (Anchor). Gunnar Myrdal, *An American Dilemma* (Harper, 1962) is still the definitive study of the plight of the Negro in twentieth-century America. To learn details about education in the South, Edgar W. Knight, *Public Education in the South* (Ginn, 1922) and J. L. M. Curry, *A Brief Sketch of George Peabody, and a History of the Peabody Education Fund* (Harvard University, 1898) are recommended. For information about Negro education, see sections of John Hope Franklin, *From Slavery to Freedom: A History of American Negroes* (Knopf, 1947).

For attitudes and points of view of Northern schoolmen, consult Merle Curti, *The Social Ideas of American Educators* (Littlefield, Adams) and Edgar B. Wesley, *NEA: The First Hundred Years. The Building of the Teaching Profession* (Harper, 1957). See also Howard K. Beale, *A History of Freedom of Teaching in American Schools* (Scribner, 1941). Albert G. Keller and Maurice R. Davie (eds.) present an elaboration of Sumner's and other "Social Darwinist" views in *Essays of William Graham Sumner* (Yale University Press, 1934). Also consult the paperback edition of Richard Hofstadter, *Social Darwinism in American Thought, 1860–1915* (Beacon).

For information about movements among the farmers, consult Solon J. Buck, *The Agrarian Crusade: A Chronicle of the Farmer in Politics* (Yale University Press, 1920), and John D. Hicks, *The Populist Revolt: A History of the Farmers' Alliance and the People's Party* (University of Minnesota Press, 1931). The definitive study of the "Myth of the Garden," is Henry Nash Smith, *Virgin Land: The American West as Symbol and Myth* (Vintage).

There are numerous paperback collections of Mark Twain's writings. See, for instance, the following editions of *The Adventures of Huckleberry Finn*: Dell, edited by Wallace Stegner; Holt, edited by Lionel

Trilling; Riverside, edited by Henry Nash Smith; and the Collier Books, Dolphin, and Penguin editions. A representative sampling can be found in Bernard de Voto (ed.), *The Portable Mark Twain* (Viking), with *The Mysterious Stranger* and other selections; and Edmund Fuller (ed.), *Mark Twain: A Laurel Reader* (Dell). Albert E. Stone, Jr., *The Innocent Eye: Childhood in Mark Twain's Imagination* (Yale University Press, 1961) is a recent study.

11. The Child and the Dynamo: Schooling in a "Gilded Age"

For a contemporary account of poverty in the period, see Jacob Riis's *How the Other Half Lives* (American Century), as well as his *The Children of the Poor* (New York, 1892). One of the definitive studies of the period is still Arthur M. Schlesinger, *The Rise of the City, 1878–1898* (Macmillan, 1933); and additional material can be found in Thomas C. Cochran and William Miller, *The Age of Enterprise: A Social History of Industrial America* (Macmillan, 1942). For useful information on immigration, see Oscar Handlin, *Race and Nationality in American Life* (Anchor). For an account of tastes and mores, see Dixon Wecter, *The Saga of American Society: A Record of Social Aspiration* (Scribner, 1937).

The works of Stephen Crane can be found in many paperback editions: for example, Austin McC. Fox (ed.), *Maggie and other Stories by Stephen Crane* (Washington Square Press); R. W. Stallman (ed.), *Stories and Tales* (Vintage); Richard Chase (ed.), *The Red Badge of Courage and Other Writings* (Riverside); and the Dolphin, Modern Library, and Collier Books editions of *The Red Badge of Courage*. William Dean Howells' *The Rise of Silas Lapham* is also in multiple paperback editions, including those issued by Modern Library, Dolphin, and Riverside. His utopian later novel, *Traveler from Altruria*, is an American Century paperback.

Horatio Alger's *Ragged Dick and Mark, the Match Boy* has been issued as a Collier Books paperback, with an introductory essay, "Horatio Alger as a Social Philosopher," by Rychard Fink. An enlightening study is John Tebbel's *From Rags to Riches: Horatio Alger, Jr. and the American Dream* (Macmillan, 1964); and, for an examination of the theme in a wider context, there is Irvin G. Wyllie, *The Self-Made Man in America: The Myth of Rags to Riches* (Rutgers University Press, 1954).

For other sorts of responses to the period, see Willa Cather, e.g., *Five Stories* (Vintage), and examples of Henry James' work, such as *Washington Square* (Bantam),*Wings of the Dove* (Dell), and some of the shorter pieces in Morton Dauwen Zabel (ed.), *The Portable Henry*

173

James (Viking). To sample the thought of Henry Adams, consult his *Degradation of the Democratic Dogma* (Capricorn), *The Education of Henry Adams* (Sentry), and *Mont-Saint-Michel and Chartres* (Anchor).

On labor and labor organization, see Terence V. Powderley's view in Harry J. Carman, Henry David, and Paul N. Guthrie (eds.), *The Path I Trod: The Autobiography of Terence V. Powderley* (Columbia University Press, 1940) and Norman J. Ware, *The Labor Movement in the United States, 1860–1895* (Vintage Caravelle).

For a study of education in New York City, see the first two chapters in Sol Cohen, *Progressivism and Urban School Reform* (Teachers College, 1963). For a representative statement of Harris' approach, see United States Bureau of Education Circular of Information No. 4, 1888, "Moral Education in the Common Schools." Edward A. Sheldon gives his views in an article entitled "Object Teaching," Mar., 1964 in the *American Journal of Education*, Vol. XIV, pp. 93–102.

For an explanation of Herbartian method, consult Charles A. and Frank M. McMurry, *The Method of the Recitation* (Macmillan, 1903), and for an example of C. Gordon Hall's thinking, see Hall's address, "The Ideal School as Based on Child Study," N.E.A. *Proceedings and Addresses* (1901). See, too, Lester F. Ward, *Dynamic Sociology, or Applied Social Science, as Based upon Statistical Sociology and the Less Complex Sciences* (New York, 1883).

12. ". . . Tomorrow We Will Run Faster. . . ."

Accounts of Progressivism and Reform are to be found in Daniel Aaron, *Men of Good Hope, A Story of American Progressives* (Galaxy); Eric Goldman, *Rendezvous with Destiny: A History of Modern American Reform* (Vintage); Richard Hofstadter, *The Age of Reform* (Vintage); Morton White, *Social Thought in America: The Revolt against Formalism* (Beacon). For contemporary articulations of "reform," see Herbert Croly, *The Promise of American Life* (Dutton Paperback), Lincoln Steffens, *The Shame of the Cities* (American Century), and Jane Addams, *Twenty Years at Hull House* (New American Library). Also consult Thorstein Veblen's *The Theory of the Leisure Class* (Mentor) and Joseph Dorfman's *Thorstein Veblen and His America* (Viking, 1934).

Representative literary responses are Frank Norris' *The Pit: A Story of Chicago* (Evergreen), Jack London, *Short Stories* (American Century), and Thedore Dreiser, *An American Tragedy* (Dell or Meridian), *Sister Carrie* (Dell or Dolphin), *The Financier* (Dell).

For selections from Charles Sanders Peirce, William James, John Dewey, and others, see Milton R. Konvitz and Gail Kennedy (eds.), *The*

American Pragmatists (Meridian). Many of Dewey's writings are in paperback; for example, *The Child and the Curriculum* (Phoenix) and *School and Society* (Phoenix); *Democracy and Education* (Macmillan); *Individualism: Old and New* (Capricorn); *Experience and Education* (Collier Books); and *Art as Experience* (Capricorn). For selections from his work, see Martin Dworkin (ed.), *Dewey on Education* (Teachers College (Classics) and Richard J. Bernstein (ed.), *On Experience, Nature, and Freedom: Representative Selections* (Liberal Arts Library). Also consult John Dewey and Evelyn Dewey, *Schools of Tomorrow* (Everyman). George R. Geiger, *John Dewey in Perspective* (Oxford, 1958) is one of many friendly overviews of Dewey's thinking. For a later, somewhat more critical view, see Oscar Handlin, *John Dewey's Challenge to Education* (Harper, 1960).

For accounts of the twentieth century history of "progressive education," see L. A. Cremin's *The Transformation of the School* (Knopf, 1961); I. B. Berkson, *Education Faces the Future* (Harper, 1943), especially Part 2; Theodore Brameld, *Education for the Emerging Age: Newer Ends and Stronger Means* (Harper, 1961); and Rush Welter, *Popular Education and Democratic Thought in America* (Columbia University Press, 1962), Part 4.

Among the numerous contemporary works presenting educational points of view, many at variance with progressivism, are the various studies by James B. Conant, including *Slums and Suburbs* (McGraw-Hill, 1961), *The American High School Today* (McGraw-Hill, 1959), and *Shaping Educational Policy* (McGraw-Hill, 1965). Raymond E. Callahan takes a fresh approach to the "business" influence on public education in his *Education and the Cult of Efficiency* (Phoenix). For a recent attempt to reconcile an old conflict, see John W. Gardner, *Excellence: Can We Be Equal and Excellent Too?* (Harper Colophon). B.F. Skinner, *Walden Two* (Macmillan Paperback) is a novelistic approach to education based on "human engineering."

To discover the challenges put to public schools by changes in urban life, see A. Harry Passow (ed.), *Education in Depressed Areas* (Teachers College, 1963); and, to identify some of these and other social changes, consult Michael Harrington, *The Other America: Poverty in the United States* (Penguin) and Nathan Glazer and Patrick D. Moynihan, *Beyond the Melting Pot* (The M.I.T. Press, 1963).

Among the many helpful studies in American literary history are: Alfred Kazin, *On Native Grounds* (Anchor) and Malcolm Cowley, *Exile's Return* (Compass), particularly for the 1920s. See also Maxwell Geismar, *The Last of the Provincials: The American Novel, 1915–1925*

(Houghton Mifflin, 1947) and Frederick J. Hoffman, *The Modern Novel in America, 1900–1950* (Regnery, 1951).

Among works of contemporary literature, the following are of particular importance: Sherwood Anderson, *Winesburg, Ohio* (Compass); Saul Bellow, *The Adventures of Augie March* (Compass); F. Scott Fitzgerald, *The Great Gatsby* (Scribner); Ernest Hemingway, *In Our Time* (Scribner); Sinclair Lewis, *Babbitt* (Signet); J. D. Salinger, *The Catcher in the Rye* (New American Library); John Steinbeck, "The Red Pony" and other stories in Pascal Covici (ed.), *The Portable Steinbeck* (Viking), and *The Grapes of Wrath* (Compass); John Updike, *The Centaur* (Crest). For a novel about a Jewish immigrant child, see Henry Roth, *Call It Sleep* (Avon). For novels about Negro life in the city, see James Baldwin, *Go Tell It On the Mountain* (Universal Library), Ralph Ellison, *Invisible Man* (Signet), and Warren Miller, *The Cool World* (Crest).